THIS BOOK
BELONGS TO

Mallory

Starr

Good Night Stories for Rebel Girls

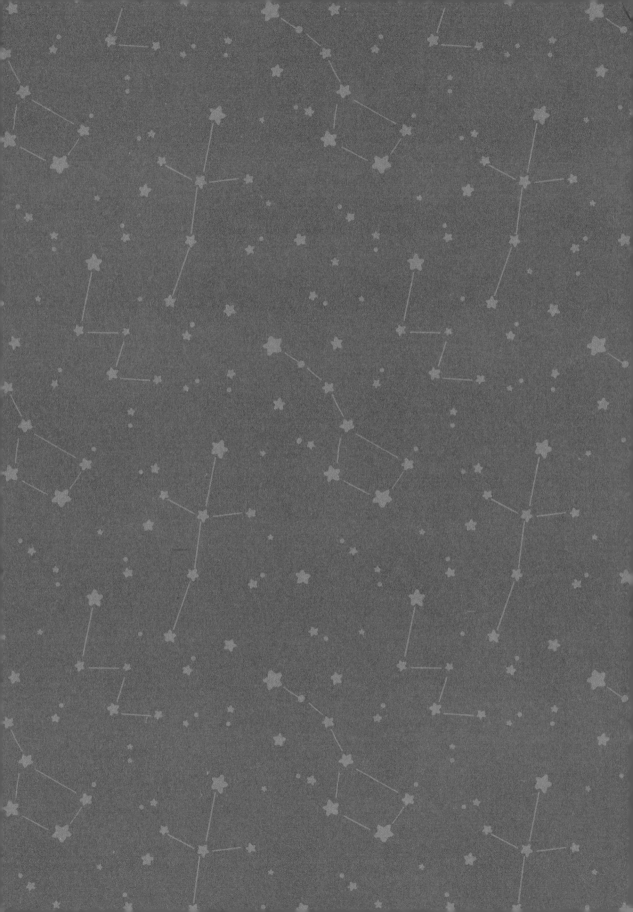

GOOD NIGHT STORIES FOR REBEL GIRLS

ELENA FAVILLI

100 IMMIGRANT WOMEN WHO CHANGED THE WORLD

REBEL GIRLS

Good Night Stories for Rebel Girls and all other Rebel Girls titles are available for bulk purchase for sale promotions, premiums, fundraising, and educational needs.
For details, write to sales@rebelgirls.com

This is a work of creative nonfiction. It is a collection of heartwarming and thought-provoking bedtime stories inspired by the life and adventures of one hundred heroic women. It is not an encyclopedic account of events and accomplishments of their lives.

www.rebelgirls.com

First Edition: October 2020
10 9 8 7 6 5 4 3 2 1

Art Director: Giulia Flamini
Graphic Designer: Annalisa Ventura
Cover Design and Lettering: Cesar Iannarella

ISBN: 978-1-7333292-9-3

Printed in Italy

Good Night Stories for Rebel Girls is FSC® certified.

MIX
Paper from responsible sources
FSC
www.fsc.org
FSC® C013123

MORE BOOKS FROM REBEL GIRLS

················

Good Night Stories for Rebel Girls

Good Night Stories for Rebel Girls 2

I Am a Rebel Girl: A Journal to Start Revolutions

Ada Lovelace Cracks the Code

Madam C. J. Walker Builds a Business

Junko Tabei Masters the Mountains

Dr. Wangari Maathai Plants a Forest

Alicia Alonso Takes the Stage

To the rebel girls of the world:

Cross boundaries

Demand freedom

Make your mark

And, when in doubt, remember

The future is yours.

CONTENTS

PREFACE

· · · · · · · · · · · · · · · · ·

Dear Rebels,

To those of you who are picking up a Good Night Stories for Rebel Girls book for the first time, I want to say, "Welcome!" And to those of you who are joining us for the second or even third time, "Welcome back!" In this book, I am excited to share with you one hundred stories of incredible women who moved from one country to another, experiencing some form of immigration over the course of their lives.

This is also a personal topic for me, as I am an immigrant myself. Good Night Stories for Rebel Girls was created by two women—me (Elena Favilli) and Francesca Cavallo—who moved from Italy to the United States and who wanted to share their vision for a more equal world with all of you. I came to the US when I was twenty-three years old to attend University of California, Berkeley. This country is now my home, where I have built this company, written these books, and met all of you. As you can see, Francesca is not writing this third book with me, but that same inspiration we shared at the start of our journey continues to drive this series.

People often ask me what it means to be a Rebel Girl, and there can be many definitions—just like we are all different from one another. At her heart, a Rebel Girl is someone who tries to make the world better for herself and the people around her, no matter the risks. In the following pages, you will read stories about women who embody the spirit of the Rebel Girl, leaving their birth countries for a multitude of reasons. Some of these women actively chose to seek new opportunities, while others left out of necessity.

You will explore the Amazon with Emilie Snethlage, part scientist, part explorer, who moved from Germany to study the plants and animals of the Brazilian rainforest. You will dance with Yuan Yuan Tan whose career as a ballerina began with the flip of a coin and brought her from China to her new home in the United States. And you will fight for what's right with Muzoon Almellehan, who fled war in Syria to settle in England, finding strength in books, campaigning for girls' education, and becoming one of the youngest UNICEF Goodwill Ambassadors to date.

Immigration is rarely thought of as a woman's story, but more than half of all immigrants are women. The women featured in this book have already made an impact on the world just by forging their own paths across borders. They also happened to accomplish great things in their new homes. But whatever an immigrant hopes to achieve through their journey, I hope you will finish this book with an understanding that movement from one country to another is a human right.

As you dive into each of these stories, it might help to think about times you've wanted to move from one place to another. Have you ever wanted to move to a different classroom? A different team? What about a different city? That is exactly what these immigrant women did, on a larger scale. Let their courage and perseverance be a reminder to you, Rebel Girls, that you should always fight for your beliefs no matter where they take you.

Yours,
Elena Favilli

ADELAIDE HERRMANN

MAGICIAN

Once upon a time, there was a girl with a flair for the dramatic. While other Victorian girls learned housekeeping skills, Adelaide practiced acrobatics, dance, and a new sport called trick cycling.

One night, Adelaide saw a magic show in London that changed her life. The magician, Alexander Herrmann (known as Herrmann the Great), asked for a volunteer, and Adelaide eagerly raised her hand. The magician set her ring on fire and made it reappear on a ribbon tied around a dove's neck!

A few months later, when Adelaide moved to New York City, she ran into Alexander again. They got married and together became one of the country's most successful magic acts. Herrmann the Great was the star, and Adelaide played supporting roles, including a dancer and a human cannonball!

In 1896, Alexander suddenly died. Adelaide was left alone with their magic show, a warehouse of props and animals, and a mountain of debt. But soon it became clear that only one person had the experience to continue Herrmann the Great's **legacy**—Adelaide herself.

For more than thirty years, Adelaide performed as the Queen of Magic. After a fire tore through her warehouse, Adelaide insisted she'd rise like a phoenix from the ashes. And she did. She continued to tour before finally retiring in her seventies.

AUGUST 11, 1853–FEBRUARY 19, 1932

ENGLAND ➜ UNITED STATES OF AMERICA

"SELF-CONFIDENCE AND ASSURANCE ARE MOST ESSENTIAL TO THE SUCCESSFUL MAGICIAN."
—ADELAIDE HERRMANN

ILLUSTRATION BY CAMILLE DE CUSSAC

ALICE GUY-BLACHÉ

FILMMAKER

Once there was a girl named Alice who spent her childhood crisscrossing the globe from France (her mother's home) to Chile (her father's home) to Switzerland (where she lived with her grandmother). When she grew up, Alice became a secretary at a camera company turned film studio. Filmmaking was a new and exciting art form. The very first films were nothing like today's movies. They showed people doing ordinary things—a group of workers simply leaving a factory or a train racing along a track.

Alice thought these films were boring and wondered: *What if film could be used to tell a story?* So she borrowed camera equipment and created her first motion picture, *The Cabbage Fairy*. It was only about one minute long, but it was one of the first films to tell a fictional story.

Eventually, Alice became the studio's head of production and experimented with new ways to make films and add special effects. She married a fellow filmmaker, Herbert Blaché, and they moved to the United States. In 1910, Alice opened her own film studio called the Solax Film Company and eventually built a state-of-the-art production studio. It was the largest film studio in the country.

Herbert became the company's president so Alice could be free to make movies. She became the world's first woman filmmaker, creating around a thousand films—many of which survive today. Alice made her last film in 1920 and was forgotten for a long time, but today's filmmakers owe a lot to this pioneering director and producer.

JULY 1, 1873–MARCH 24, 1968
FRANCE ➔ UNITED STATES OF AMERICA

ILLUSTRATION BY
HELEN LI

"THERE IS NOTHING
CONNECTED WITH THE STAGING
OF A MOTION PICTURE THAT
A WOMAN CANNOT DO
AS EASILY AS A MAN."
—ALICE GUY-BLACHÉ

ANGELICA ROZEANU

TABLE TENNIS PLAYER

Once upon a time, there was a young Romanian, Jewish girl who was a natural athlete, but she didn't have a favorite sport—at least, not at first. Angelica loved swimming, tennis, and cycling. But one day, as Angelica later described it, a new sport found her.

When she was around eight years old, Angelica got scarlet fever. Scarlet fever was a serious illness, and it took a long time to get better. Angelica's brother, Gaston, wanted to find a way to entertain his sister as she recovered. He brought home a paddle, ball, and net, and introduced Angelica to table tennis.

Angelica was a quick learner. With dancer-like footwork and quick reflexes, she began to play competitively and won her first national championship when she was fifteen! In 1940, however, her athletic career suddenly stopped. Romania joined forces with Nazi Germany. As a result of the many restrictions put on Jewish people in Romania at the time, Angelica was unable to play the sport she loved.

When the war ended, Angelica once again picked up her paddle. In 1950, she became the first Romanian woman athlete to win a world championship. That year, she also became president of the Romanian Table Tennis Commission. Over her career, Angelica won at least fifteen national championships and seventeen world championships. In 1960, after experiencing more **discrimination** in her home country, Angelica **immigrated** to Israel. In 1981, Angelica was inducted into the International Jewish Sports Hall of Fame.

OCTOBER 15, 1921–FEBRUARY 21, 2006
ROMANIA → ISRAEL

"I PREFERRED TABLE TENNIS
OR PERHAPS, IF YOU LIKE,
TABLE TENNIS PREFERRED ME."
—ANGELICA ROZEANU

ILLUSTRATION BY
MAGGIE COLE

ANITA SARKEESIAN

JOURNALIST AND MEDIA CRITIC

Anita loved video games. As a little girl growing up in Canada, she begged her parents for a Nintendo Game Boy of her own. When she was in high school, she spent hours playing on the computer. Video games were fun, and they made her happy.

But as she got older, she noticed something that bothered her. There were hardly any female game characters—and extremely few strong, positive female ones.

This wasn't the first time Anita had noticed something amiss in the media. When she was younger, Anita had seen that people from Iraq—the country her parents were from—were often portrayed on television as scary or bad. She didn't see any representations that looked like the people she loved. Anita realized that sometimes the media told stories that weren't accurate or left important things out.

Anita started her own website, a blog called *Feminist Frequency*. She posted a series of videos in which she talked to viewers about the way women were depicted in video games.

Her videos were smart and funny, and made people in the gaming industry think about how to make their products better for men and women alike. But some men who saw the videos didn't want to hear any new ideas. They called her ugly names. Some even threatened to hurt her.

Anita refused to be silent, and the more she spoke up, the more people listened. Today there are more women than ever in video games—both as characters on the screen and as engineers designing them.

ILLUSTRATION BY
JENNY MEILIHOVE

"THERE IS SO MUCH VALUE
TO SPEAKING UP FOR WHAT
YOU BELIEVE IS RIGHT,
EVEN IF THE COSTS FEEL
INSURMOUNTABLE."
—ANITA SARKEESIAN

ANNA WINTOUR

EDITOR IN CHIEF

Once there was a girl who had a style all her own. From a young age, Anna was captivated by the world of fashion. It called to her from the glossy pages of magazines and the vibrant London streets where she lived. Anna's father, a respected newspaper editor, encouraged his daughter's interests. With his help, Anna got her first job at a high-end boutique when she was fifteen years old. Shortly afterward, she started taking fashion design classes. But she quickly grew tired of them. *You either know fashion or you don't,* she thought. And it was clear: Anna *knew* fashion.

At twenty, Anna got her first job at a fashion magazine. For the next few years, she worked at many different magazines in London and New York. In 1988, Anna was hired for the job that made her famous in the fashion world. She became editor in chief of *Vogue*. Right away, Anna was determined to follow her instincts. For her very first cover, she had a model wear a $10,000 jeweled top with a pair of ordinary jeans. It was so unusual that at first some people thought it was a mistake. But Anna wasn't afraid to try new things.

Thirty years later, Anna is still the editor in chief of *Vogue*. Although she is known for her trademark look—a bob haircut and oversized sunglasses—she is more than simply a style icon. Her bold ideas, take-charge attitude, and focus on **philanthropy** have helped change the world of magazines and fashion for the better.

BORN NOVEMBER 3, 1949

ENGLAND ➝ UNITED STATES OF AMERICA

"PEOPLE RESPOND WELL
TO SOMEONE WHO'S SURE
OF WHAT THEY WANT."
—ANNA WINTOUR

ANNE HIDALGO

POLITICIAN

Born in San Fernando, Spain, Ana Maria Hidalgo and her family moved to France when she was a child. They lived in a working-class neighborhood full of fellow immigrants. Ana Maria grew up speaking two languages—Spanish to her parents and French to most everyone else. As a teenager, Ana Maria changed her name to Anne and became a French **citizen**. Today she has both French and Spanish citizenship.

In school, Anne studied social services and law, planning to one day work in government. After moving to Paris, she worked in civil service for many years and eventually became deputy mayor in 2001. Anne spent thirteen years as deputy mayor, working for the people of Paris. But she wanted to do more.

In the 2014 elections, Anne ran for mayor. Some people didn't think she would win because of her immigrant background, but more people seemed to think this experience made her a good candidate—and they were right. She won the election! For hundreds of years, Paris had been an important center for politics, business, art, and fashion, and it had had many leaders—from military generals to kings to mayors. But no woman had ever been in charge, until Anne.

Since taking office, Anne has championed climate change issues. She wants to help create a greener world, and she knows the importance of starting right where you are: "My vision for Paris is as a green city where we can all breathe fresh air, share open space, and enjoy our lives."

BORN JUNE 19, 1959

SPAIN ➞ FRANCE

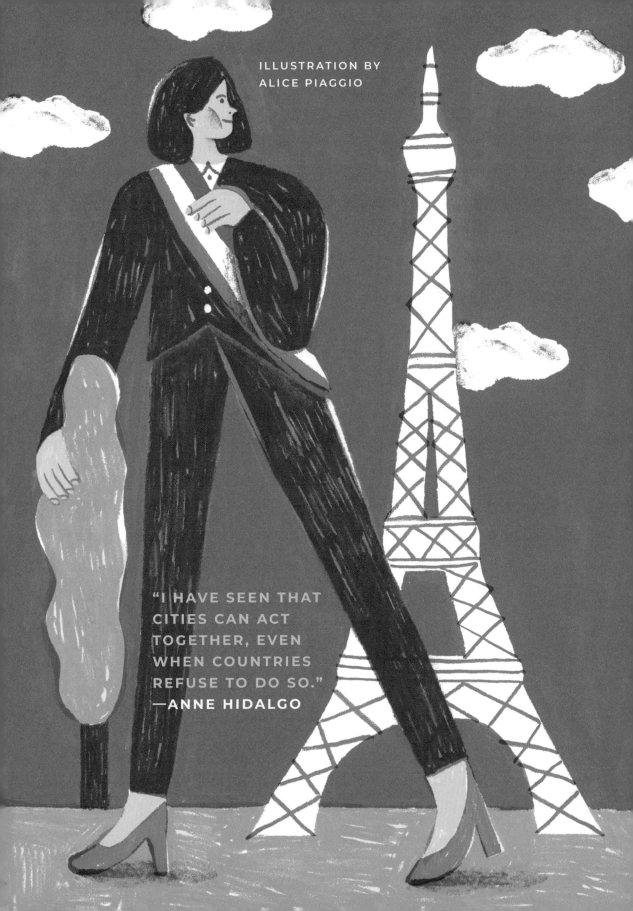

ILLUSTRATION BY
ALICE PIAGGIO

"I HAVE SEEN THAT
CITIES CAN ACT
TOGETHER, EVEN
WHEN COUNTRIES
REFUSE TO DO SO."
—ANNE HIDALGO

ANNE WAFULA STRIKE

PARALYMPIAN

One day in Kenya, a two-year-old girl named Anne became very, very sick. Her worried parents took her to a hospital, where doctors wrapped her in stiff plaster that made it impossible to move. When Anne got better, she could no longer walk. She had contracted polio and was paralyzed from the waist down.

Many people in Anne's village did not understand what polio was. The local healer said she was a victim of evil magic. Her neighbors called her a snake because she had to crawl everywhere to get around.

Her body worked differently now, but Anne refused to stop moving. She learned to use crutches, and her father found a special school that taught children with disabilities. Anne excelled at school. She became the first person in her family to go to university.

Later, when Anne was working as a teacher in Kenya, she fell in love with a fellow teacher named Norman. They decided to get married and move to Essex, England, where Norman was from.

One day, while exercising at her local track, a coach noticed Anne circling the track in her wheelchair and asked if she had ever tried competitive racing. It turned out that Anne was fast—very fast. Two years later, in Athens, Anne became the first wheelchair racer from east Africa to compete in the Paralympic Games.

In 2006, Anne became a British **citizen**. The next year, she won a bronze medal at the Paralympic World Cup before a cheering crowd as an athlete competing for her new home—Great Britain.

BORN MAY 8, 1969
KENNA ➜ GREAT BRITAIN

ILLUSTRATION BY
LUISA RIVERA

"I CONSIDER MYSELF
AN ESSEX GIRL FROM AFRICA."
—ANNE WAFULA STRIKE

ANNIKA SÖRENSTAM

GOLFER

Once upon a time in Sweden, there was a girl who didn't want to sit on the sidelines. Annika was a confident athlete who played tennis and soccer, and raced down the slopes as an Alpine skier. When she was twelve, she started playing golf at summer camp. "I was determined to figure it out," Annika said.

Annika eventually joined a team and became a very good golfer. But there was a problem. In the junior tournaments, the winners gave victory speeches. Annika was shy, so she lost on purpose, getting second place instead of first. Annika's coaches noticed. They had the rules changed, so both the winner and runner-up had to give speeches. Annika decided that if she had to give a speech either way, she might as well win!

After high school, Annika played golf for the University of Arizona. She won the NCAA tournament as a college freshman, and a year later, she left school to be a professional golfer.

Over the next two decades, Annika became one of the most successful female golfers of all time. She won ninety tournaments, was inducted into the World Golf Hall of Fame, and was the first woman to play on the PGA Tour in its fifty-eight year history. The year before she retired, Annika started her own brand and a foundation to introduce girls to golf. "My goal now is to inspire others to pick up the game," Annika said.

ILLUSTRATION BY
KATERINA VORONINA

"I DON'T PLAY FOR FAME
OR ACCOLADES.
FOR ME, IT'S ALL ABOUT
PERFORMANCE AND
SATISFACTION."
—ANNIKA SÖRENSTAM

ARIANNA HUFFINGTON

AUTHOR AND CEO

Once there was a girl named Arianna who read everything she could find, and nothing could distract her: not the neighborhood kids calling her to play or the trucks at the fire station across the street from her family's apartment in Athens.

When she was just sixteen, Arianna moved to England and eventually won a scholarship to attend Cambridge University. Some of the other students made fun of her Greek accent when she spoke. But Arianna refused to be silent. Instead, she spoke up more, first as president of Cambridge's famous debating club and later in her life as a journalist and TV commentator.

Arianna moved to the United States in 1980 and eventually cofounded a website, the *Huffington Post*, to share the viewpoints and ideas from people all over the world. As she grew her business, Arianna also continued to write books, make speeches, and advocate for causes she cared about. She often worked eighteen hours a day and hardly ever slept!

Then came a day that changed Arianna's life. One minute she was busy returning emails and making phone calls. The next she was on the floor. She had collapsed, and the fall broke her cheekbone and cut open her face. She went to see doctors who told her she had exhaustion. If she didn't change her hectic schedule, she was going to get very sick.

Arianna adjusted her life to make sure that her health came first. Later, she started a new company, Thrive Global, that teaches people how to care for themselves while doing the work they love.

BORN JULY 15, 1950
GREECE ➔ UNITED STATES OF AMERICA

"WE THINK, MISTAKENLY, THAT SUCCESS IS THE RESULT OF THE AMOUNT OF TIME WE PUT IN AT WORK, INSTEAD OF THE QUALITY OF TIME WE PUT IN."
—ARIANNA HUFFINGTON

ILLUSTRATION BY FANNY BLANC

ASMA KHAN

· · · · · · · · · · · · · · · ·

CHEF

One day in India, a girl stood on a magnificent fortress that had belonged to her **ancestors**. Her father pointed at the slums below. "It is an accident of birth," he said. "You could have been there, or you could have been here. Use your life to make a difference, because being in a position of privilege, you have a duty. To lift others up."

But Asma didn't feel powerful. She was a second-born daughter. In India, sons were so important that a second daughter was often a disappointment. She vowed to make her family proud.

Asma eventually married and moved to England, where she earned her PhD in law. She was terribly homesick. As Asma passed a neighbor's house, she smelled the familiar foods of her childhood. Asma longed to cook these recipes herself. She took a trip to India and asked her mother to teach her.

When Asma returned to London, she hosted supper clubs in her home. She became friends with other South Asian immigrant women and invited them to cook with her. Their dinners became so popular that Asma opened her own restaurant, which specialized in homestyle Indian food. But food was just one part of Asma's mission. She also wanted to empower women. She started a nonprofit to celebrate the births of second daughters in India and began employing an all-women staff in her restaurant. Many were second-born daughters like Asma. "I've watched these women grow, stand tall, be proud," Asma said. "This is what happens to women when other women stand by them."

BORN CIRCA JULY 1969

INDIA ➜ ENGLAND

"WE NEED TO UNITE TO PROTECT THE RIGHTS OF THE NEXT GENERATION OF WOMEN AND WOMEN TODAY WHO ARE STRUGGLING."
—ASMA KHAN

ILLUSTRATION BY PAOLA ROLLO

BANA ALABED

ACTIVIST

Once there was a happy girl who lived in the city of Aleppo, Syria, and her name was Bana. Bana loved to swim with her father, make up songs and games with her friends, and explore the beautiful flowers in her family's garden.

When Bana was two, her world began to change. War broke out in Syria. There was fighting in the streets and she couldn't play outside anymore. Many of her friends and relatives moved away to different countries. Some of them were hurt or even killed. Bana and her family felt sad, alone, and very afraid.

A few years later, her own city was attacked. For weeks, bombs fell on Aleppo. Bana and her family couldn't get food, water, or medicine. They desperately needed help. With the assistance of her mother, Fatemah, Bana posted messages on Twitter. Though it was difficult and dangerous, Bana bravely reported her experiences to the public. On days when their internet wasn't working, neighbors would invite them over to use theirs, in the hopes that the world would understand what ordinary people were facing in Aleppo and help them.

Eventually, Bana and her family had to leave Syria and start a new life in Turkey. At first, Bana was scared to go to a new country, but when she got there, she saw that there was no war. She could go to school again, and she was so happy.

Bana wants to be a teacher when she grows up. "I want to change everything," Bana said. "I don't want war anymore."

BORN CIRCA JUNE 2009

SYRIA ➜ TURKEY

"DO WHAT YOU CAN DO AND BELIEVE IN YOURSELF BECAUSE YOU MAKE THE FUTURE."
—BANA ALABED

ILLUSTRATION BY TATHEER SYEDA

CARMEN HERRERA

ARTIST

Growing up in Havana, Cuba, with six siblings and two journalist parents, Carmen loved to draw. She went to college to study architecture but stayed only one year. There were lots of protests in Cuba, and the university was often closed. But at architecture school, Carmen said later, "an extraordinary world opened up to me that never closed: the world of straight lines."

Carmen got married and moved with her husband to New York, where he lived. All the while, Carmen made art—bold, bright geometric paintings and sculptures. Though other artists admired her work, she never got to show her paintings in museums and galleries the way male artists did.

Carmen eventually sold her first painting in 2004, when she was eighty-nine years old. At an age when many artists put away their easels and retired, Carmen was just getting started.

Every morning, Carmen took a seat before the big, beautiful window in her New York City apartment. She picked up her sketchbook and drew whatever inspired her: the lines and angles of the shadows, the memory of a landscape.

After decades as a painter, Carmen reached the peak of her artistic fame. Museums around the world showed her work, and she kept painting every day, well after her one hundredth birthday. After all, why should she stop? "I've painted all my life," she said. "It makes me feel good."

BORN MAY 30, 1915

CUBA ➔ UNITED STATES OF AMERICA

ILLUSTRATION BY
MAÏTÉ FRANCHI

"I NEVER MET A STRAIGHT LINE
I DID NOT LIKE."
–CARMEN HERRERA

CARMEN MIRANDA

SINGER AND ACTRESS

Maria do Carmo Miranda da Cunha was born in a small town in Portugal. But by the time she moved to Brazil as a baby, her father had given her a nickname, Carmen, after the famous opera.

Carmen dreamed of a career in show business and recorded some of her first albums singing popular Brazilian songs.

After her first hit record, in 1930, Carmen became a star in Brazil, singing and dancing her way through a series of movie musicals. By 1939, she created her signature look: colorful flowing dresses, platform shoes, and elaborate headdresses.

In June 1939, Carmen and her band performed in a Broadway show. American audiences were captivated by her. Carmen's next stop was Hollywood, where she made more than a dozen films and became the highest-paid actress in the country.

But as Carmen's international success grew, she became less popular back home. Some Brazilians thought she encouraged stereotypes of Latinx people and that she wasn't a true Brazilian because she hadn't been born there. She responded by recording a defiant song in Portuguese called "Disseram Que Eu Voltei Americanizada" ("They Say I've Come Back Americanized"). Through her perseverance and resilience, Carmen showed that a person can be more than one thing and be from more than one place.

FEBRUARY 9, 1909–AUGUST 5, 1955
PORTUGAL → BRAZIL AND UNITED STATES OF AMERICA

ILLUSTRATION BY
SONIA LAZO

"I INVENT MY HATS, I INVENT
MY SHOES, I INVENT MY DRESS.
I HAVE THE IDEAS FOR MY
SONGS, AND I KNOW EXACTLY
WHAT PEOPLE LIKE."
—CARMEN MIRANDA

CAROLINA GUERRERO

JOURNAL IST AND PRODUCER

Once there was a girl named Carolina who always wanted to learn something new. In Colombia, where she grew up, she taught people how to scuba dive. When she moved to New York City, she became an art dealer and designer. Later, she organized workshops, art shows, and cultural festivals all over North and South America.

The world was so rich and full, Carolina thought. How could anyone limit themselves to just one place, one language, one **culture**?

In her new home in New York City, Carolina loved to listen to radio programs that told deep, important stories about things she would otherwise never have known about. But these programs were only in English. What about the people, like herself, who spoke Spanish? Why wasn't there a place where they could tell their stories, in their own language?

Carolina decided to start a podcast of her own. *Radio Ambulante* would be a storytelling podcast by and for Spanish speakers. Once a week, the podcast would introduce listeners to firefighters in Peru or punk rockers in Mexico, astronomers in Argentina or soccer stars in Brazil. Carolina became the CEO, the person responsible for making sure *Radio Ambulante* grew and thrived as a business.

The first show was shared in 2011, and today millions of people around the world listen in every week. With *Radio Ambulante*, Carolina brings people together through the power of storytelling.

COLOMBIA ➔ UNITED STATES OF AMERICA

CHINWE ESIMAI

FINANCIAL EXECUTIVE

Once there was a girl who believed it was more important to shine bright than blend in. When Chinwe was a teenager, her family moved to the United States from Nigeria. In the US, Chinwe realized the way she looked and spoke made her stand out—and not always in a positive way. She also noticed that other immigrants—especially women of color—often tried to disappear into the crowd.

Chinwe eventually earned a degree from Harvard Law School. In her work as a lawyer and later as a professor, she noticed the same troubling thing: immigrant women sometimes downplayed their differences in order to succeed. One of her students was an immigrant from China who never spoke in class even though she was very smart. The student didn't think she should speak up or try to lead until her accent had faded. But Chinwe believed cultural differences—including her own—were strengths. She wanted other women to believe it, too.

Chinwe started a leadership website and blog. It was a place where immigrant women could find advice to help them become leaders, especially in the business world. Chinwe wrote from her own experience. Eventually, she became a managing director and chief anti-bribery and corruption officer at an investment banking company where she was the first person to hold that title. And she did it all without hiding who she was. Chinwe said, "I think it's very important to view our background and our **culture** as a positive because that's something unique that you bring to the table."

ILLUSTRATION BY
D'ARA NAZARYAN

"EVERYONE'S VOICE
IS IMPORTANT."
—CHINWE ESIMAI

CLARA JULIANA GUERRERO LONDOÑO

BOWLER

There was no place Clara loved more than the bowling alley, and no sound she loved more than the heavy *crash!* of a ball knocking down all ten pins at once. Clara's grandfather, parents, and brother all loved to bowl. By the time Clara was nine, she was a bowler, too. And she was really good at it, winning bigger and bigger tournaments as time went on.

But at Clara's first national tournament for young bowlers, she had a bad game and lost. So she vowed to work even harder.

By the time she was eighteen, Clara had made the Colombian national bowling team. She was one of the best bowlers in her country and was even voted the sport's Amateur Athlete of the Year. Still, Clara had bigger dreams. The largest bowling tour in the world was in the United States, and the best college bowling team in the US was at Wichita State University.

Moving to a brand-new country would be a challenge, but Clara was willing to try it. It paid off: with Clara on the roster, Wichita State won the national championships!

Clara graduated in 2006 with a degree in international business— and an even better game. In 2009, after winning two gold medals at the women's world championships, Clara was voted Bowler of the Year by the World Bowling Writers. She was also named Athlete of the Year in Colombia—the first time a bowler had been awarded that honor.

BORN APRIL 22, 1982
COLOMBIA ➜ UNITED STATES OF AMERICA

ILLUSTRATION BY AMALTEIA

"MOVING TO A NEW COUNTRY WITH A DIFFERENT CULTURE FAR AWAY FROM HOME TO FOLLOW YOUR DREAM HELPS MAKE YOU STRONGER AS A PERSON." —CLARA JULIANA GUERRERO LONDOÑO

CLARA LEMLICH SHAVELSON

ACTIVIST

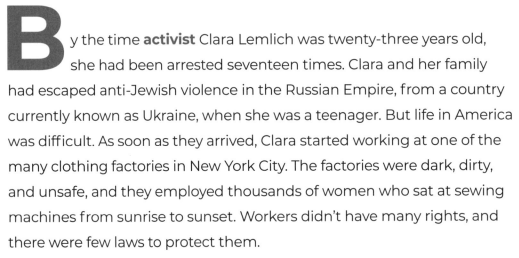

By the time **activist** Clara Lemlich was twenty-three years old, she had been arrested seventeen times. Clara and her family had escaped anti-Jewish violence in the Russian Empire, from a country currently known as Ukraine, when she was a teenager. But life in America was difficult. As soon as they arrived, Clara started working at one of the many clothing factories in New York City. The factories were dark, dirty, and unsafe, and they employed thousands of women who sat at sewing machines from sunrise to sunset. Workers didn't have many rights, and there were few laws to protect them.

Americans had started to form unions—groups of workers who band together—which they believed would give them a voice to fight for their rights. At the time, most unions were led by men and didn't let women get involved. But Clara insisted that unions needed women in order to succeed. Clara organized her fellow workers, wrote articles, and asked people to strike. One day, she gave a passionate speech in **Yiddish** at a union meeting. Her speech led to a huge labor strike that brought about important changes such as better wages and working conditions.

Clara was unfairly arrested over and over for her activism, but she never backed down. She worked hard on causes like women's **suffrage** and helped renters who had unfair landlords. Her passion for justice among working-class people shaped her entire life.

MARCH 28, 1886–JULY 12, 1982
UKRAINE ➔ UNITED STATES OF AMERICA

"I THINK THE WOMEN WHO BUY AND WEAR THE BEAUTIFUL CLOTHES DO NOT KNOW HOW IT IS FOR THE GIRL WHO MAKES THEM.... OR THEY WOULD CARE AND WOULD TRY TO HELP HER."
—CLARA LEMLICH SHAVELSON

ILLUSTRATION BY LISA LANOË

CLAUDIA RANKINE

POET AND PLAYWRIGHT

Once there was a seven-year-old girl named Claudia whose family left their tropical island home for a new life in New York City.

Life in crowded, gritty New York City was very different from life in Jamaica. Claudia's mother wanted her to be proud of being Jamaican, but Claudia also wanted to fit in. She looked like other black Americans, but she didn't share some of their **culture**. Claudia spent a lot of time reading and thinking about her new world. Eventually, she would turn these thoughts into stories and poems.

Later, Claudia earned college degrees in literature and poetry and began to teach at a university. She continued to watch, listen, and write. In 1994, she published her first poetry collection. Since then, Claudia's poetry has won many important awards, and she's written several plays. In 2014, one of her books became the first book of poetry to ever hold a place on the *New York Times* bestseller list for nonfiction.

But Claudia doesn't write poetry for the awards. Instead, she sees her poems as conversations with her reader. These conversations are often about difficult topics, like **racism**. But Claudia believes that hard conversations can lead to understanding. "It's our job to see the person in front of us," she said, "and if that means having an uncomfortable conversation, have that conversation. Please."

BORN CIRCA 1963

JAMAICA ➜ UNITED STATES OF AMERICA

ILLUSTRATION BY
NICOLE MILES

"I WASN'T WAITING TO BE
CHOSEN—YOU DON'T WRITE
WITH THE FREEDOM THAT I DO
IF THAT'S WHAT IS ON YOUR MIND."
—CLAUDIA RANKINE

DANIELA SCHILLER

NEUROSCIENTIST

Once there was a girl who was curious about how the brain worked. Daniela had always loved complicated questions. As a child in Israel, she spent hours in her backyard mixing concoctions and exploring what would happen when she added *this* to *that*.

But there were some questions Daniela couldn't answer. For a sixth-grade class project, she tried to interview her father about his experiences during the **Holocaust**, but his memories were too painful to share.

She wanted to understand why fear and painful memories were so powerful. So she became a scientist who studied the part of the brain that controlled emotion and memory. She also wanted to help people like her father who had lived through terrible things. After getting her PhD in cognitive neuroscience, Daniela moved to the United States and got a job with an important research lab. Scientists were learning how to use medication to change the way people felt about their bad memories. They would no longer cause fear, sadness, or pain.

Later, Daniela made her own amazing discovery: it was possible to change bad memories *without* using medication. She realized if a person experienced something pleasant while thinking about a bad memory, that would help change how they felt about it. Since that discovery, Daniela has continued to study the brain and is now the leader of her own research lab. Her groundbreaking work is being used to bring healing and hope to people who—like her father—are living with trauma and anxiety.

BORN OCTOBER 26, 1972
ISRAEL ➔ UNITED STATES OF AMERICA

ILLUSTRATION BY
IRENE RINALDI

"WE AREN'T A SLAVE
TO OUR PAST. IF YOU
ARE STUCK WITH A BAD
MEMORY…IT'S NOT
EXACTLY THE TRUTH
AND YOU CAN REVISE IT."
—DANIELA SCHILLER

DANIELA SOTO-INNES

CHEF

Once there was a girl who believed that food should bring people joy. It was a lesson she learned in her family's kitchen in Mexico. Daniela spent her childhood helping her grandmother in her bakery and learning recipes from her mother. "I knew it was the thing that made me the happiest," she said.

When Daniela was twelve years old, her family moved from Mexico City to Texas. Two years later, she got her first restaurant job and attended culinary school soon after. But when Daniela started working in restaurants, she was disappointed by what she saw: kitchens were not joyful places. The staff worked long hours, and the chefs were harsh bosses. Daniela decided that if she ever ran a restaurant, she would do things differently.

She didn't have to wait long. Her career as a chef started in Mexico City, and when Daniela was just twenty-four, she was asked to lead a Mexican-inspired restaurant in New York City. The restaurant became a huge success, and it allowed Daniela to combine both her Latin American and American roots in experimental ways.

In 2016, Daniela won the James Beard Award for Rising Star Chef. Eventually, she opened another restaurant and has won even more awards. To Daniela, her greatest success is the community she's created and a staff that feels like family. Her kitchens are always full of laughter, dancing, and singing—just like in the kitchen of her childhood.

BORN AUGUST 26, 1990

MEXICO → UNITED STATES OF AMERICA

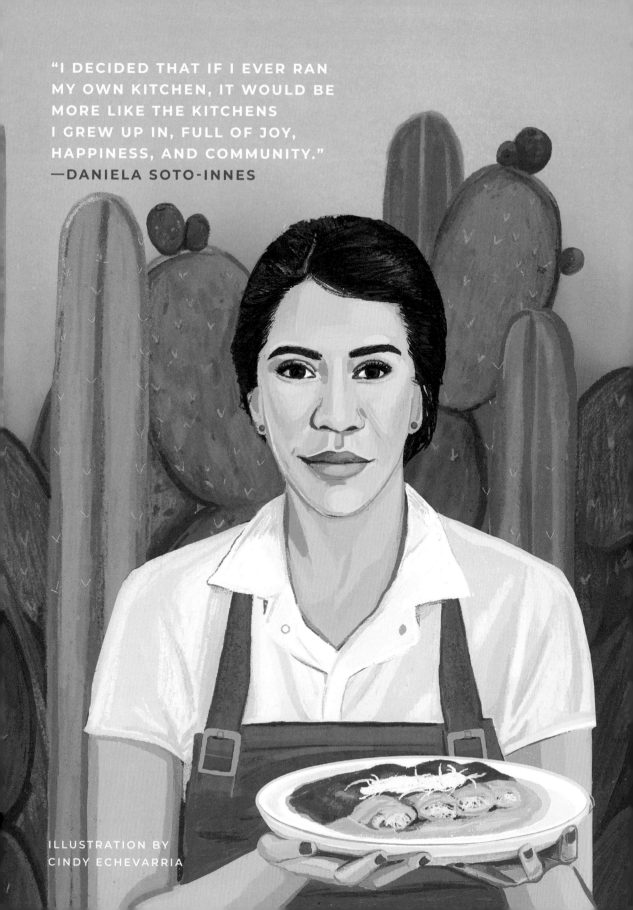

"I DECIDED THAT IF I EVER RAN MY OWN KITCHEN, IT WOULD BE MORE LIKE THE KITCHENS I GREW UP IN, FULL OF JOY, HAPPINESS, AND COMMUNITY."
—DANIELA SOTO-INNES

ILLUSTRATION BY CINDY ECHEVARRIA

DAPHNE KOLLER

COMPUTER SCIENTIST AND ENTREPRENEUR

Once upon a time, there was a girl named Daphne who loved to learn. She loved math and computers, and started programming when she was twelve years old. When she was a young teenager, Daphne told her parents she was bored in high school. She wanted to go to college instead.

Daphne was only seventeen years old when she graduated from university in Israel. Soon after, she decided to move to the United States to get her PhD. Daphne arrived on July 4, 1989. It was Independence Day in the US—a good day, she decided, to start a life in her new country.

By studying artificial intelligence and centuries-old ideas about decision-making, Daphne found new ways to teach computers to make predictions. Her research helped doctors figure out how cancer spreads, how to prevent illness in premature babies, and other lifesaving work.

Because of her own experiences in school, Daphne also knew the importance of a flexible education. She wanted to connect students with the knowledge they craved, even if they didn't have money or means to get to a classroom.

With her business partner, Daphne started Coursera, a company that would allow people all over the world to take university classes online. Since then, Daphne has been elected to the American Academy of Arts and Sciences and named one of the world's most influential people by *Time* magazine.

ILLUSTRATION BY
FANNY BLANC

"THE WORLD IS NOISY
AND MESSY. YOU NEED
TO DEAL WITH THE
NOISE AND UNCERTAINTY."
—DAPHNE KOLLER

DIANE VON FÜRSTENBERG

FASHION DESIGNER

In fairy tales, when a woman becomes a princess, she lives happily ever after in a castle. But when a young Belgian woman named Diane married a German prince, she didn't want to live a sheltered life. She wanted to *do* something. "I decided to have a career," she said. "I had to be someone of my own."

After Diane von Fürstenberg and her husband moved to the United States and had two children, she started to design her own clothing line: Diane von Fürstenberg Studio. One day, Diane combined a wrap-style shirt and skirt into a simple long-sleeved dress that tied at the waist: a wrap dress. The design was a success. Made from soft fabric with no zippers or buttons, the wrap dress was comfortable and easy to wear. It was a style that was formal enough for office work but fashionable enough to wear after work, too. In 1975, Diane's studio made fifteen thousand wrap dresses a week, and by 1976, she had sold more than five million dresses!

Today Diane von Fürstenberg owns one of the most successful fashion empires in the world. Her designs are worn by women everywhere, including royalty and movie stars. Diane also uses her success to mentor and help other women. "I did not know what I wanted to do," Diane said, "but I knew the kind of woman I wanted to be."

BORN DECEMBER 31, 1946
BELGIUM → UNITED STATES OF AMERICA

"I WANT TO EMPOWER
EVERY WOMAN."
—DIANE VON FÜRSTENBERG

ILLUSTRATION BY
ELISA SEITZINGER

DOREEN SIMMONS

SPORTS COMMENTATOR

Once upon a time, there was a girl who dreamed of seeing what life was like in a country different from her own. After college, she traveled far from home—first to Singapore and then to Japan. In Japan, Doreen became captivated by the country's favorite sport: sumo wrestling.

Growing up in England, Doreen had loved to watch a sport called cricket. She watched it every Saturday and took careful notes about what she saw. Years later, when Doreen learned about the complicated world of sumo wrestling, she did the same thing. She became an expert.

"I took up sumo watching just like I did cricket, taking notes with my own homemade scorecard—oh, and learning Japanese frantically," Doreen said.

Doreen traveled all over Japan to watch tournaments and wrote a magazine column about sumo. It was rare for a woman—especially a woman who wasn't Japanese—to be part of the inner world of sumo, but Doreen was not afraid to do the unexpected. In 1992, she was hired as a part-time commentator for sumo matches on national TV in Japan. She helped viewers understand what they were seeing. The TV network depended on Doreen for her expert knowledge. In 2017, the Japanese government awarded Doreen with the Order of the Rising Sun, one of the country's highest honors, to celebrate her contributions to Japan's **culture**.

MAY 29, 1932–APRIL 23, 2018
ENGLAND ➜ JAPAN

"EVERYTHING IN MY LIFE CHANGED FROM BLACK AND WHITE TO GLORIOUS COLOR. AND I'VE BEEN LIVING IN GLORIOUS COLOR EVER SINCE."
—DOREEN SIMMONS

ILLUSTRATION BY PETRA BRAUN

EDMONIA LEWIS

SCULPTOR

Once upon a time, there was a little girl called Wildfire. Born in New York to an Afro-Haitian father and a mother who was Mississauga Ojibwe, Wildfire became an orphan at a young age and was taken in by her mother's sisters.

When Wildfire was a young woman, she dropped her Ojibwe name and started to use her other given name, Mary Edmonia Lewis—or just Edmonia, for short. Edmonia attended one of the first American colleges that allowed students of color, but she experienced terrible **racism** there. She was even falsely accused of poisoning two white classmates and put on trial. The jury decided that Edmonia was innocent, but she was forced to leave college without graduating.

Around 1863, Edmonia moved to Boston to become a sculptor. In those days, people thought sculpting was only for men.

As the first American woman of color to become a professional sculptor, Edmonia attracted attention from white **abolitionists**. But she dreamed of living in a place where people paid more attention to her skill than to her **ethnicity**.

Around 1865, Edmonia moved to Rome and joined a community of artists. In 1876, she created a sculpture of Cleopatra in honor of America's one hundredth anniversary. Sadly, most of Edmonia's art hasn't survived, but this sculpture did. It disappeared for a century until it was discovered in a Chicago mall covered in paint, and it now lives at the Smithsonian American Art Museum.

CIRCA 1844–SEPTEMBER 17, 1907

UNITED STATES OF AMERICA → ITALY

"I HAVE A STRONG SYMPATHY FOR ALL WOMEN WHO HAVE STRUGGLED AND SUFFERED."
—EDMONIA LEWIS

ILLUSTRATION BY
MONICA AHANONU

EILEEN GRAY

ARCHITECT AND FURNITURE DESIGNER

Once there was a girl named Eileen who left Ireland to study drawing at a famous London art school. As she wandered the streets one day, she ducked into a shop where craftspeople were repairing old lacquer screens. Seeing her excitement, they eventually invited her to help out. And so, Eileen traded her drawing pencils for tools when she discovered a new passion: furniture design.

A few years later, Eileen moved to Paris to study art and learn from Japanese lacquer master Seizo Sugawara. The two artists opened a workshop together, and people began to buy Eileen's unique and eye-catching furniture. She loved to experiment with unexpected materials like glass, chrome, and steel tubes, and challenge old design methods. Eileen eventually opened her own gallery, where she sold her furniture, light fixtures, and handwoven carpets.

Over time, Eileen's interest changed from furniture design to modern architecture. She read architecture books, took drafting lessons, and joined architects at their building sites. She also drew plans of her own. Eileen's first—and most famous—building was a villa she called E-1027. The house was white and rectangular like a row of sugar cubes and was perched on a cliff overlooking the Mediterranean Sea. It was filled with Eileen's modern furniture. Eileen continued to work and create until she died at age ninety-eight. By then she had gained the reputation as a pioneer in the modern design movement.

AUGUST 9, 1878–OCTOBER 31, 1976
IRELAND ➡ LONDON AND FRANCE

"TO CREATE, ONE MUST FIRST QUESTION EVERYTHING."
—EILEEN GRAY

ILLUSTRATION BY
JOSEFINA SCHARGORODSKY

ELENA PONIATOWSKA

JOURNALIST

Once upon a time, there was a girl named Elena who was born to a wealthy family in France descended from Polish royalty.

When Elena was around nine years old, her family moved to Mexico to escape World War II. She wanted to learn more about her new home and the people who shared it with her. One of the best ways to do that was to become a reporter. It was a reporter's job to pay attention, write things down, and ask questions—and Elena loved asking questions! She got her first job at a newspaper when she was twenty-one.

Elena was drawn to stories that other writers overlooked: those of poor people, Indigenous people, prisoners, and women. She wrote dozens and dozens of works, including essays, nonfiction books, articles, novels, poetry, and books for children.

Elena also told stories that other journalists were too afraid to write about. When soldiers attacked peaceful **protesters** in Mexico City in 1968, Elena was brave enough to write about it. Though she was threatened, Elena believed that her book about the attack should be published. It was published all over the world and became a bestseller, helping survivors and their families understand what happened that night. When the government tried to give her a prize for the book, she refused it. The people they should be honoring, she said, were the victims.

In 2014, Elena won the Cervantes Prize, the highest honor for writing in the Spanish language.

BORN MAY 19, 1932

FRANCE ➡ MEXICO

ILLUSTRATION BY
CRISTINA MARTÍN

"I WAS ALWAYS ASKING
TOO MANY QUESTIONS, AND
I'LL BE THAT WAY UNTIL I DIE."
—ELENA PONIATOWSKA

ELISA ROJAS

When a girl named Elisa was born, the doctors were worried. Something was different about this baby, they said. Her body was shaped differently. Some of her bones broke at birth.

Her parents did not care. When they looked in Elisa's eyes, all they saw was a smart and spirited girl looking back at them.

Elisa was born with a genetic condition that made her bones break easily. She would always need to use a wheelchair to get around. But Elisa was bright and curious, and did not see why that should stop her from chasing her dreams. Her parents didn't, either. The family moved from Chile to a new home in France so Elisa could have better opportunities: not just for her medical care but for her brilliant mind, too.

Elisa excelled in school and decided to become a lawyer. She passed her exams, but it took eighteen months to find a law firm willing to hire a woman who used a wheelchair.

Elisa was a great lawyer, but practicing law wasn't always easy. She often arrived at courthouses to represent her clients to find that she was not able to get into the building. Elisa was furious. She had the right to access those places just as much as any other person in France. Her disability wasn't the problem. The problem was people's refusal to treat her as an equal.

Elisa helped form a group that fought to make laws fair for people with disabilities. She is still fighting today.

BORN APRIL 30, 1979
CHILE ➡ FRANCE

"WE WANT SIMPLE RESPECT FOR OUR RIGHTS."
—ELISA ROJAS

ILLUSTRATION BY
ANNALISA VENTURA

ELISABETH KÜBLER-ROSS

PSYCHIATRIST

One summer night in Switzerland, three tiny girls were born right in a row: Elisabeth, Erika, and Eva. From the beginning, Elisabeth was determined to make her own way in the world. Even before she finished school, Elisabeth knew she wanted to be a doctor. Her bold plans made her father angry, so at sixteen years old, Elisabeth left home, working odd jobs and volunteering in wartime hospitals.

In 1951, Elisabeth went to medical school in Switzerland to become a psychiatrist. After marrying a fellow doctor, Elisabeth moved to the United States. At her new job in a hospital, she worked with patients who were sick with illnesses that could not be cured. She was shocked by how these patients were treated. The medical staff seemed to know very little about death and how to talk about it. Elisabeth believed that death was a normal part of life and that people should be able to talk about it in honest ways. She convinced the hospital to allow her to provide counseling and care for the patients.

For the rest of her career—as a psychiatrist, professor, and author—Elisabeth taught medical students, doctors, and nurses to be honest and compassionate toward dying patients. She developed the well-known theory of the five stages of grief, and her work changed many attitudes in the medical community. Her work inspired the creation of a hospice system, special clinics that care for terminally ill patients. In 2007, Elisabeth was inducted into the National Women's Hall of Fame for her pioneering work.

JULY 8, 1926–AUGUST 24, 2004

SWITZERLAND ➔ UNITED STATES OF AMERICA

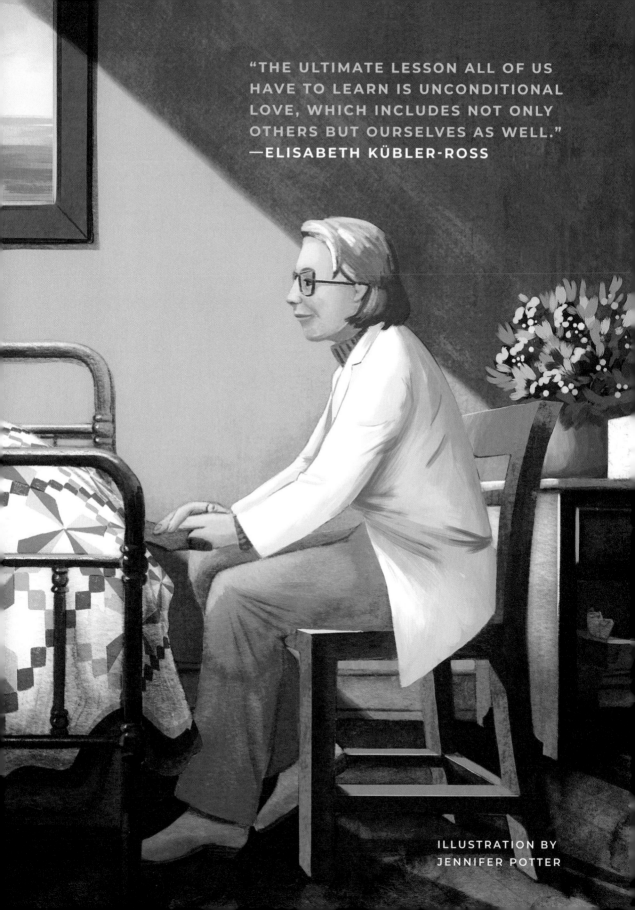

"THE ULTIMATE LESSON ALL OF US HAVE TO LEARN IS UNCONDITIONAL LOVE, WHICH INCLUDES NOT ONLY OTHERS BUT OURSELVES AS WELL."
—ELISABETH KÜBLER-ROSS

ILLUSTRATION BY JENNIFER POTTER

ELIZABETH NYAMAYARO

POLITICAL SCIENTIST

Once upon a time, there was a girl who dreamed about working for the United Nations. Elizabeth was eight years old when a terrible famine happened in Zimbabwe. But, one day, help arrived. A young woman in a blue uniform came to her village and handed out food. She told Elizabeth, "As Africans, we must all uplift each other." The woman worked for the United Nations, an organization that encourages countries to work together to solve problems and help people.

After a second famine struck, Elizabeth was sent to live in Harare, Zimbabwe's capital, with an aunt she'd never met. At ten years old, Elizabeth started attending school, where she experienced inequality and **prejudice** for the first time. Because she couldn't speak English and was behind in reading and writing, her classmates looked down on her. It was a difficult experience. But it also made Elizabeth more determined to help others who were mistreated.

Elizabeth later left Zimbabwe to study political science in London. After graduation, her childhood dream came true: she got a job at the United Nations! As a senior director there, Elizabeth helped launch an important worldwide movement for gender equality called HeForShe. The movement encouraged men and women to work together to speak out against stereotypes and **discrimination**. Elizabeth made a home for herself in New York but dreams of returning to Africa one day. She even started a nonprofit to help people there. "Africa has given me so much and made me who I am," Elizabeth said. "I want to be part of the solution."

ZIMBABWE → UNITED STATES OF AMERICA

"IT'S BEEN A LONG ROAD TO GET TO WHERE I AM NOW."
—ELIZABETH NYAMAYARO

ILLUSTRATION BY MARIAN BAILEY

EMILIE SNETHLAGE

. . . .

ORNITHOLOGIST

When Emilie attended the University of Berlin for the first time around age thirty, she was an eager student. She wanted to study natural history.

Despite being a bright student, Emilie unfortunately was also an invisible one. Women weren't allowed to officially enroll in college yet in Germany, so Emily had to sit behind a screen when she attended class. Despite this unfair treatment, Emilie earned her doctorate in 1904 and began her career as a zoological assistant at the Berlin Natural History Museum.

But a bigger adventure was waiting. In 1905, Emilie was hired to be a zoological assistant at Museu Paraense Emílio Goeldi, a museum and research institution in Belém, Brazil. When she boarded the boat for her journey, it was the first time she had traveled so far outside her own country.

From then on, Brazil was Emilie's home. Part scientist, part explorer, she studied the animals of the Amazon, and she trekked to remote parts of the rain forest to collect specimens. Emilie became best known for her work as an ornithologist, a scientist who studies birds. In 1914, she became the first woman director of a scientific institution in South America. She also published a book about Amazonian birds that was 530 pages long! At least five animal species, including two bird species, have been named in her honor.

. . . .

APRIL 13, 1868–NOVEMBER 25, 1929

GERMANY ➜ BRAZIL

ILLUSTRATION BY
BODIL JANE

"I KNOW THE BIRDS
SO WELL, THAT I KNOW
WHAT KIND OF BIRD IS
IN FRONT OF ME EVEN
BEFORE IT LANDS."
—EMILIE SNETHLAGE

EMMY NOETHER

MATHEMATICIAN

Once there was a girl whose mind came alive whenever she studied math. In Emmy's day, women were not welcome in college classrooms in Germany. She had passed exams that would have allowed her to teach English and French to girls, but Emmy didn't want to follow that path.

In 1904, the University of Erlangen allowed women students for the first time, and Emmy enrolled immediately. By 1907, she had earned her PhD in mathematics. For the next seven years, Emmy taught at that same university alongside her father, who was also a mathematician.

Because of unjust rules about women teachers, the university refused to pay Emmy, but she earned the respect of other mathematicians during that time, including two of her former teachers. One day, those teachers asked for Emmy's help. They were struggling with some problems related to Albert Einstein's new theory of relativity. In the process of working with them, Emmy proved a new mathematical result. It's known today as Noether's theorem, and it's an important part of physics. She also helped start a new branch of mathematics called abstract algebra.

Around 1923, Emmy began teaching at the University of Göttingen. She was devoted to her classes, but when the Nazis came to power in Germany ten years later, the university fired all professors who were Jewish like Emmy. Emmy left for the United States, and today she's considered one of the most important mathematicians of the twentieth century.

MARCH 23, 1882–APRIL 14, 1935
GERMANY ➡ UNITED STATES OF AMERICA

"MY METHODS ARE REALLY
METHODS OF WORKING
AND THINKING."
—EMMY NOETHER

FATMA IPEK ALCI

ACTIVIST

Once upon a time, there was a nurse named Fatma who moved from Turkey to Sweden so she could use her skills to take care of sick people there.

The first neighborhood where she and her family lived was a very nice place. Then her daughter got sick, and when the local hospital couldn't help her anymore, Fatma's family moved to Stockholm, the capital of Sweden, which had a bigger hospital.

The new neighborhood was very different. It wasn't safe. Young people were getting into trouble, damaging markets and other local businesses. Some people were afraid to leave their houses.

Fatma didn't think this was right. She cared about her new community, so she met with other parents to try to figure out how to fix the problems. Under Fatma's direction, they organized teams of local neighbors to walk around the area at night to help everyone feel safe.

She also realized that young people were getting into trouble because there was nothing for them to do. She convinced the government to open a job center for teenagers in their area, which helped. She even started taking classes in private security herself.

In 2017, Fatma was named Hero of the Year by a Swedish newspaper for her work in the community.

"WE HAVE TO SAVE OUR YOUTH....
I'M NOT A COP, BUT I'M A MOTHER,
I'M A GRANDMOTHER, I'M AN AUNT.
I THINK ABOUT MY GRANDKIDS,
MY NEIGHBORS' CHILDREN."
—FATMA IPEK ALCI

FRIEDA BELINFANTE

CELLIST AND CONDUCTOR

Once there was a girl named Frieda who lived and breathed music. Her father was a professional pianist, so it was no surprise that Frieda was a natural musician. She played the cello from a young age and eventually set out to become a professional musician like her father. Things didn't exactly go as planned. After graduating from a conservatory in Amsterdam in 1921, Frieda applied to be a high school music teacher. The school hired a man instead, believing he'd be better at disciplining students. Ultimately, that frustrated teacher quit, and Frieda was hired in his place. She was a capable teacher and—quite unexpectedly—a talented conductor. The head of Amsterdam's royal concert hall asked Frieda to be the conductor and artistic director for their chamber orchestra, making her the first woman conductor of a chamber orchestra in Europe.

World War II interrupted Frieda's career. She bravely joined the Dutch **resistance** even though she was of Jewish heritage and a lesbian. After being pursued by the Nazis, Frieda disguised herself as a man and escaped to Switzerland by crossing the Alps on foot.

After the war, Frieda **immigrated** to the United States and became a music professor at the University of California, Los Angeles. She also became the conductor and artistic director of the Orange County Philharmonic. As director, she insisted the concerts have free admission so more people could hear their music. "I pioneered in music," Freida said when she was in her nineties. "I liked that, to bring music where it wasn't."

MAY 10, 1904–APRIL 26, 1995

NETHERLANDS ➜ UNITED STATES OF AMERICA

ILLUSTRATION BY
GOSIA HERBA

"I'VE ALWAYS BEEN
A PERSISTENT PERSON.
I DON'T TAKE NO FOR
AN ANSWER. IF IT CANNOT
BE DONE, I WOULD SAY,
'WE'LL SEE.'"
—FRIEDA BELINFANTE

GERALDINE COX

HUMANITARIAN

Once there was a girl named Geraldine who longed to experience life outside her small Australian town. She finally got to travel abroad when she was nineteen years old and spent a year working as a secretary in a London office. When she returned to Australia, her desire to know more about the world was even stronger.

At age twenty-six, Geraldine worked for Australia's Department of Foreign Affairs and was assigned to the office in Phnom Penh, Cambodia. This changed the course of her life. At that time, Cambodia was experiencing a bitter civil war. In the years that followed, Geraldine's job sent her all over the world: to the Philippines, Thailand, and Iran. In Cambodia, meanwhile, millions suffered under a brutal dictator named Pol Pot. Geraldine followed this news with a heavy heart and longed to return. She cared deeply about the country and its people.

When she was fifty years old, Geraldine moved back to Cambodia and volunteered at an orphanage. The war and Pol Pot were long gone, but the country was still very poor and recovering from years of hardship.

Then more fighting broke out. The orphanage workers were scared, but Geraldine refused to leave behind the sixty children living there. She founded her own orphanage, Sunrise Cambodia, to help children whose families couldn't care for them. She even set up schools and training programs. Over the years, thousands of children in Cambodia have called Sunrise home. They call Geraldine *M'Day Thom*—Big Mother.

BORN CIRCA 1945

AUSTRALIA ➡ CAMBODIA

"EVERYONE WANTS
TO BE NEEDED."
—GERALDINE COX

GERALDINE HEANEY

ICE HOCKEY PLAYER AND COACH

A screaming crowd filled the arena at the gold-medal game between Canada and the United States at ice hockey's first-ever women's world championships. A Canadian named Geraldine got the puck and fired so hard that her body flew through the air—just as the game-winning goal sailed into the net.

Geraldine was born in Northern Ireland. When she was just a baby, her parents decided to move the family to Canada. When they arrived, they learned their new country was passionate about a sport called ice hockey.

As soon as she was old enough to skate, Geraldine followed her older brothers to the ice rink so she could play, too. Not many girls played ice hockey. But Geraldine didn't care. She just loved to play. By the time she was thirteen, she had signed with a semiprofessional women's team. Within a decade, she'd be a member of the women's national team.

During her time on Canada's national team, Geraldine won seven world championships, a silver medal at the 1998 Olympics, and a gold medal at the 2002 Olympics, her final international tournament. She was only the third woman to be inducted into the Hockey Hall of Fame.

Geraldine played her last professional game in 2004, at the Canadian national championship. Just as she had almost fourteen years earlier, Geraldine scored the game-winning goal to win the gold. This time, however, she was three months pregnant with her first child.

After Geraldine stopped playing ice hockey professionally, she became a coach, passing on her love of the game to other young women.

BORN OCTOBER 1, 1967

NORTHERN IRELAND → CANADA

"I WAS TOLD, 'GIRLS DON'T PLAY HOCKEY'.... BUT I JUST IGNORED ALL THAT."
—GERALDINE HEANEY

ILLUSTRATION BY
PAOLA ROLLO

GERDA TARO

PHOTOGRAPHER

O nce there was a fearless girl who used her camera to tell the truth about the world. Gerta Pohorylle grew up in Germany, but she was forced to flee after the Nazis came to power. At twenty-three, she moved to Paris, where she met and fell in love with a fellow Jewish **refugee**, Endre Friedmann. Endre was an adventurous photojournalist, and as Gerta worked as his assistant, he taught her all he knew. Soon, Endre and Gerta were working as a team and traveled to Spain to photograph the Spanish Civil War.

Gerta and Endre faced a lot of **prejudice** due to political intolerance and anti-Semitism in Europe. Together, they invented an alias, a fake American photographer they called Robert Capa to avoid **discrimination** and to command higher prices for their work. At first, Gerta and Endre both published their photos under this name. After a while, however, only Endre used the name Robert Capa, while Gerta published under the name Gerda Taro.

The couple traveled through Spain and to the front lines of the civil war. They took photos of soldiers and refugees, and documented how the violent war hurt ordinary people. Gerta was a bold photographer, and traveled to increasingly dangerous places. In 1937, tragedy struck: Gerta died while photographing the Battle of Brunete. She is considered the first woman war photographer to die in battle. In Paris, over ten thousand people lined the streets to pay their respects at her funeral and honor her bravery.

AUGUST 1, 1910–JULY 26, 1937

GERMANY ➡ FRANCE

GLORIA ESTEFAN

SINGER

Once there was a shy girl who grew to love the spotlight. When Gloria's family left Cuba in 1959, there was a **revolution** happening there. They built a new life in Florida, where Gloria and her siblings went to school, her mother got a job, and her father volunteered to fight in the Vietnam War. When he returned, he was very sick.

Gloria spent her teen years taking care of her father. During this difficult time, her love of music grew. "When my father was ill, music was my escape," Gloria said. Gloria's love of singing eventually led to the stage. She met a fellow Cuban immigrant named Emilio, who asked her to join his band.

Gloria and Emilio soon got married, and eventually, Gloria became a solo artist. She sang in English and Spanish, becoming popular in the US and overseas. In 1990, however, Gloria's music career nearly ended. The band's tour bus got into an accident, and Gloria was badly hurt. Doctors told her she might never walk again. But less than a year later, she was back onstage.

Gloria and Emilio became a powerful force in music and in business. Between them, they have released more than twenty albums, won twenty-six Grammys, and produced a musical. They own a recording studio, a publishing company, restaurants, hotels, and part of a football team! In 2017, Gloria received the Kennedy Center Honors for her contributions to American **culture**. She was the first Cuban American to ever receive the award.

BORN SEPTEMBER 1, 1957

CUBA ➜ UNITED STATES OF AMERICA

"MUSIC IS MY FIRST LOVE."
—GLORIA ESTEFAN

ILLUSTRATION BY
NAN LAWSON

GOLDA MEIR

POLITICIAN

Once there was a girl who was born to be an **activist**. When Golda was in school, she noticed that some students didn't have textbooks because they couldn't afford them. Golda rallied her friends to hold a fundraiser to buy textbooks for their classmates. She and her family had **immigrated** to the US only a few years ago. They had left their home in the Russian Empire, from a country currently known as Ukraine, because Jewish people were no longer safe there.

In America, Golda trained to become a teacher and taught **Yiddish** at a school in Milwaukee. She also joined a group of political activists who believed Jewish people should have their own country in the Middle East where their **ancestors** had first lived. Eventually, Golda and her husband, Morris Meyerson, moved to the Middle East themselves and joined a community called a kibbutz.

In 1948, Golda was one of two women to sign Israel's declaration of independence. For over two decades, she worked in Israel's government. When she was asked to take a Hebrew last name, she changed it from Meyerson to Meir, which means "illuminate."

When she was about sixty-eight, Golda wanted to retire, but people urged her not to. Then one day, Israel's prime minister unexpectedly died, and Golda, then secretary-general, became prime minister. A few months later, her political party won the election, and she served as prime minister for four and a half more years. She was Israel's fourth prime minister and, to this day, the only woman prime minister Israel has had.

MAY 3, 1898–DECEMBER 8, 1978

UKRAINE ➔ UNITED STATES OF AMERICA AND ISRAEL

"IT ISN'T REALLY IMPORTANT
TO DECIDE…EXACTLY WHAT
YOU WANT TO BECOME WHEN
YOU GROW UP. IT IS MUCH MORE
IMPORTANT TO DECIDE ON THE
WAY YOU WANT TO LIVE."
—GOLDA MEIR

HANNAH ARENDT

PHILOSOPHER AND POLITICAL THEORIST

Once there was a girl with a brilliant mind who wasn't afraid to ask puzzling questions. Her name was Hannah, and by the time she was a teenager, Hannah knew ancient Greek, had read many classic books, and had memorized many German and French poems.

Hannah went to a university where she learned how to think big and ask hard questions. She studied a subject called philosophy, which is the study of knowledge, right and wrong, and the way people think. In 1929, Hannah earned her PhD in philosophy and wanted to become a professor so she could help other people become deep thinkers, too.

But in 1933, Hannah was thrown into prison. She had been researching the Nazi Party and their plans to harm Jewish people. When Nazi officials found out, they arrested her.

After she was released, Hannah escaped to France and then **immigrated** to New York City as a **refugee**. She eventually became a professor and taught at some of the top American universities. Hannah wrote political philosophy books that examined topics such as the struggle between good and evil. One of her most important theories attempted to explain how ordinary people can get swept up in governments and political systems that do evil things. It was something she had tried to understand in her own country as she watched her fellow Germans join the Nazis. Hannah's deep thinking and writing made her one of the most important philosophers of the century.

OCTOBER 14, 1906–DECEMBER 4, 1975
GERMANY → FRANCE AND UNITED STATES OF AMERICA

ILLUSTRATION BY
ALESSANDRA
DE CRISTOFARO

"THE SAD TRUTH IS THAT
MOST EVIL IS DONE BY
PEOPLE WHO NEVER MAKE
UP THEIR MINDS TO BE
GOOD OR EVIL."
—HANNAH ARENDT

HAZEL SCOTT

MUSICIAN AND ACTIVIST

Once upon a time, there was a girl named Hazel with a special gift for music. Hazel's mother was a pianist and a music teacher, and whenever one of her students hit a wrong note, Hazel would scream as if she were hurt.

One day, when she was three years old, Hazel climbed up on the piano bench and tapped out a favorite song on the keys, without ever being taught. It turned out she had a perfect ear for music and couldn't stand to hear a note played wrong.

Soon she moved with her mother and grandmother from their home in Trinidad to New York City in search of more opportunities. When she auditioned at the Juilliard School, one of the world's most famous music schools, the professor who heard her play said she was a genius. He even gave her a special scholarship. Juilliard didn't usually take students until they were sixteen—and Hazel was only eight!

Jazz, blues, classical: Hazel could sing and play it all. She soon became famous, and used her celebrity to fight back against the **discrimination** that black people faced. When she was asked to appear in Hollywood movies, she refused to do roles or wear costumes that were demeaning to black women. When she toured, she refused to play for **segregated** audiences.

"Why would anyone come to hear me...and refuse to sit beside someone just like me?" she said. Newspapers said she had "a style all her own."

JUNE 11, 1920–OCTOBER 2, 1981
TRINIDAD ➡ UNITED STATES OF AMERICA

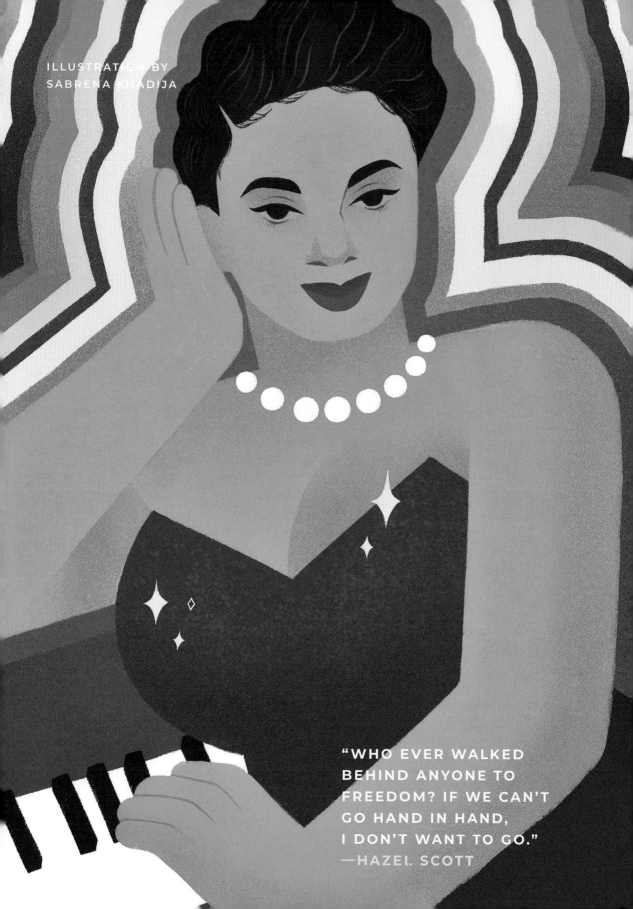

ILLUSTRATION BY
SABRENA KHADIJA

"WHO EVER WALKED
BEHIND ANYONE TO
FREEDOM? IF WE CAN'T
GO HAND IN HAND,
I DON'T WANT TO GO."
—HAZEL SCOTT

ILHAN OMAR

POLITICIAN

Once there was a small girl in Somalia whose grandfather told her a secret: she had the spirit of a mighty queen, like Somalia's legendary Queen Arawelo. This made the girl, Ilhan, feel proud.

When Ilhan was about eight years old, a war broke out in Somalia. Rockets flew near her home, and a few even hit her house. Her family fled to a **refugee** camp in Kenya, and four years later, they found **asylum** in a new country: the United States. There, Ilhan and her family settled in Minnesota. Ilhan was different from many of the kids at her school because she was black, and a refugee, and Muslim.

Ilhan's grandfather explained to her that America was a democratic country, which meant that everyone could have a voice in their government, no matter their differences. She was fascinated by the way politics could change people's lives for the better.

Ilhan became an American **citizen** when she was seventeen years old. After she graduated from college, she worked on political campaigns before deciding to run for office herself. In 2016, she won a seat in Minnesota's state government. Two years later, she ran for US Congress—and won. Ilhan became the first Somali American woman to serve as a US representative. When she flew to Washington, DC, to be sworn in, she landed at the same airport where she'd arrived as a refugee.

Though some people criticize Ilhan's ideas, she isn't afraid to speak up for what she believes is right. Thanks to her, many more people have their voice represented in America's democracy.

BORN OCTOBER 4, 1982
SOMALIA ➜ KENYA AND UNITED STATES OF AMERICA

ILLUSTRATION BY
ALESSANDRA
DE CRISTOFARO

"THE FLOOR
OF CONGRESS
IS GOING TO LOOK
LIKE AMERICA."
—ILHAN OMAR

INDRA DEVI

YOGI

Eugenie was a girl who felt at home everywhere in the world. Her father was from Sweden, and her mother was from Russia. She was born in Latvia, and when she was a young woman, she moved to Germany, where she became an actor and dancer.

But one place called to her more than anywhere else: India. She was fascinated by the country's poetry, its **culture**, and, most of all, yoga, a spiritual practice that involved meditation, breathing exercises, and poses that calmed a person's body and mind. At the time, yoga was mainly practiced in India. In the Soviet Union, it was even banned. Eugenie wanted to know more about it.

In 1927, she sailed to India, and three years later she met a famous guru, or teacher, named Sri Tirumalai Krishnamacharya. The first time she asked him to teach her yoga, he said no. Mostly men practiced yoga, and he wouldn't teach a woman. But she persisted, and eventually he agreed. Eugenie decided to adopt a new name in her new home: Indra Devi.

It did not take long for Sri Krishnamacharya to see that Indra was a special student who could share yoga with the world. She moved all over—to China, to the United States, to Mexico, and eventually to her adopted home of Argentina.

Indra called yoga the "art and science of living." Her many admirers around the world called her *mataji*, which means "mother" in Hindi.

"IN MEDITATION,
YOU ASK FOR NOTHING.
YOU JUST CONTEMPLATE."
—INDRA DEVI

ILLUSTRATION BY
JOSEFINA SCHARGORODSKY

JAWAHIR JEWELS ROBLE

REFEREE

Once there was a girl in London who played soccer every chance she had. Never mind the skirts and hijab she wore, or her parents' disapproval—she knew she belonged on the soccer field. Jawahir—known as JJ—had learned to play soccer on the streets of Mogadishu, where she sometimes used a potato as a soccer ball. When JJ's family fled Somalia because of civil war and moved to England, her love of soccer was one thing in her life that didn't change.

As a teenager, JJ's love of soccer led to an unexpected opportunity. One day, she was asked to referee for a junior league soccer game. JJ loved the challenge so much that she decided to make it her career.

In soccer, as in most sports, referees need to be quick thinkers and confident. As the first female Muslim soccer referee in the United Kingdom, JJ also had to overcome **prejudice** and **racism**. Players were often surprised to see that their referee was a small Somali woman wearing a hijab. "I don't let that stop me from doing my work," JJ said. "Refereeing is a tough job, there is a lot of pressure, you have to be focused and make quick decisions, so I don't have time to think about what people think of me."

JJ quickly advanced from refereeing youth games to adult games. She won awards for her work and has used her influence to encourage other Muslim girls to play soccer. She has set a goal for herself to be a referee at the 2023 Women's World Cup. "It would be a dream come true," JJ said.

BORN CIRCA 1994

SOMALIA ➡ ENGLAND

"IT'S GOOD TO STRETCH YOURSELF,
TO TEST YOURSELF. DECISION-MAKING,
BEING STRONG: YOU LEARN SO MANY
VALUES FROM BEING A REF."
—JAWAHIR JEWELS ROBLE

JOSEPHINE BAKER

ENTERTAINER AND ACTIVIST

Once there was a girl who dazzled audiences in Paris with her jeweled skirts and spectacular dancing.

As a young black girl growing up in the United States, Josephine cleaned houses and babysat to earn money, and she was sometimes treated with cruelty and ignorance by the white people she worked for. Eventually she joined a vaudeville troupe and toured the country as an entertainer. Then when she was nineteen years old, Josephine left for France, where her amazing career as a singer, dancer, and actor took off. She officially became a French **citizen** in 1937.

During World War II, Josephine used her fame and talents to help fight the Nazis. She charmed German officials, passed information to the **Allies**, and carried private messages for the **resistance** in invisible ink on her music sheets. The French government later made her a knight of the Legion of Honor, its highest award for bravery.

After the war, Josephine visited the United States. She was angry to see that black people there still faced the same **discrimination** she had as a girl. She stood alongside Martin Luther King Jr. and made a speech to a spellbound audience before the March on Washington in 1963.

"I have walked into the palaces of kings and queens and into the houses of presidents...," she said. "But I could not walk into a hotel in America and get a cup of coffee, and that made me mad. And when I get mad, you know that I open my big mouth. And then look out, 'cause when Josephine opens her mouth, they hear it all over the world."

JUNE 3, 1906–APRIL 12, 1975
UNITED STATES OF AMERICA ➜ FRANCE

ILLUSTRATION BY
TYLA MASON

"WHEN I SCREAMED LOUD ENOUGH,
THEY STARTED TO OPEN THAT DOOR
JUST A LITTLE BIT, AND WE ALL STARTED
TO BE ABLE TO SQUEEZE THROUGH IT."
—JOSEPHINE BAKER

JUDY CASSAB

PAINTER

A girl named Judy picked up a paintbrush for the first time when she was twelve years old. She loved art, and when she painted, she was putting her feelings on canvas for all the world to see.

But then World War II came to Europe, and Judy's family's life was in danger because they were Jewish. Judy had to leave art school and live under a false identity to avoid being captured. When the war was over, she was saddened by the destruction she saw around her. She wanted to paint only beautiful things.

In 1951, Judy and her husband, Jancsi Kampfner, moved with their two young sons to Australia. The family lived in a crowded boarding house with many other immigrants, and it was hard to find work. But Judy was determined to make art. She started painting portraits of businesspeople and their families in Australia. When word of her talent spread, she started traveling around the world to paint portraits of royals and other famous people.

Judy painted beautiful landscapes and abstract images, but she also loved portraying people. When people came to her studio to sit for a portrait, she asked them questions about themselves. She wanted to know what they were like on the inside as well as the outside.

In 1967, Judy became the first woman artist to twice win Australia's top prize for portraiture.

AUGUST 15, 1920–NOVEMBER 3, 2015

AUSTRIA → AUSTRALIA

"THE EYES ARE WHERE I RETURN ALWAYS, LIKE A SHIP TO THE LIGHTHOUSE."
—JUDY CASSAB

ILLUSTRATION BY CECILIA PUGLESI

JULIETA LANTERI

PHYSICIAN AND POLITICIAN

Once there was a girl who believed that women and men were equal, even when laws said they were not. Julieta's family **emigrated** from Italy to Argentina when she was young, and Julieta quickly discovered that her new country had just as many challenges as her old one.

Julieta was smart and determined. She was the first girl to enroll in her postsecondary school and later went to college *and* medical school. However, she was told that women shouldn't have careers, and she couldn't participate in some of the activities in medical school classes. She was also discriminated against because she was an immigrant.

After Julieta became a doctor, she applied to be a professor at the medical school, but she was rejected because she wasn't a citizen. In order to apply for citizenship in Argentina, a woman usually had to be married. And even once Julieta was married and became a **citizen** in 1911, she was not allowed to vote.

Julieta worked hard to change unfair laws. As a doctor, she helped people who didn't have access to medicine and people who had mental illnesses. She also became a politician and boldly spoke up for women's **suffrage** and other causes. She even started her own political party— the National Feminist Union. Sadly, Julieta died in a car accident in 1932. Fifteen years later, women got the right to vote in Argentina, and when they did, it was thanks to the work of brave women like Dr. Julieta Lanteri.

MARCH 22, 1873–FEBRUARY 25, 1932

ITALY ➡ ARGENTINA

ILLUSTRATION BY
KIKI LJUNG

"WOMEN MUST FIGHT
TO ACHIEVE THE REALIZATION
OF THEIR RIGHTS."
—JULIETA LANTERI

KAREN CORR

BILLIARDS PLAYER

Once upon a time, there was a girl who wanted a spot at a certain kind of table. Karen liked to tag along with her father when he went to the local pub in their town in Northern Ireland. When they got there, Karen's eyes always went to a green table in the corner. It was a table for snooker, a game similar to billiards, or pool.

When Karen was eight, her family moved to England. Her brother and her father joined a local snooker club. By the time she was fourteen, Karen didn't want to just stand on the sidelines and watch anymore. She was ready to learn to play and insisted she be allowed to join the club, too.

As it turned out, Karen was good at snooker—very good. She loved its quiet power, how a single quick movement of the cue stick sent balls spinning in many different directions.

She entered her first professional tournament less than a year later and made it to the final rounds. When she was twenty-one, she won the World Ladies Snooker Championship, then won it two more times in the coming years.

It was hard to earn a living playing snooker in the UK, even as one of the best players in the world. So Karen switched her game to pool and moved to the United States, where professional pool players could earn much bigger prizes. Within a few years, Karen was ranked as the number one women's pool player in the world. In 2012, Karen, whose nickname became the Irish Invader, was named to the Billiard Congress of America Hall of Fame.

BORN NOVEMBER 10, 1969

NORTHERN IRELAND ➔ ENGLAND AND UNITED STATES OF AMERICA

ILLUSTRATION BY
AKVILE MAGICDUST

"WHEN I WON THE NATIONALS,
I WAS SO HAPPY THAT I JUMPED
ON TOP OF THE POOL TABLE
AND DID AN IRISH JIG!"
—KAREN CORR

KAREN HORNEY

PSYCHOANALYST

omen had only been legally allowed to attend university in parts of Germany for six years when Karen announced in 1906 that she was going to medical school. Her parents hated the idea—medical school was no place for a proper young woman! Karen didn't care.

While at university, Karen gave birth to her first child and both her parents died within a year. It was a lot to deal with at once. Throughout this difficult time, Karen received psychological counseling, which sparked her interest in psychoanalysis—mental health treatment where doctors help patients explore their thoughts, emotions, and fears.

Eventually, Karen taught psychoanalysis and treated patients in Berlin. The most famous psychoanalyst at that time was a man named Sigmund Freud, but he misunderstood women, saying they were just jealous that they couldn't be more like men!

Karen thought this was ridiculous. Women were human beings with feelings of their own. In her writing, Karen focused on how the **cultures** people grew up in could affect the way they thought about themselves—something that was true for men and women alike.

By the early 1930s, Karen was at odds with Freud and his followers in Germany, and worried by the Nazi Party's rise to power. She **immigrated** to the United States and found a home in New York City. Today she is recognized as a trailblazer in feminine psychology.

SEPTEMBER 16, 1885–DECEMBER 4, 1952
GERMANY ➡ UNITED STATES OF AMERICA

"LIKE ALL SCIENCES
AND ALL VALUATIONS,
THE PSYCHOLOGY
OF WOMEN HAS HITHERTO
BEEN CONSIDERED ONLY
FROM THE POINT
OF VIEW OF MEN."
—KAREN HORNEY

ILLUSTRATION BY
LUISA RIVERA

KARIN SCHMIDT

MUSHER AND VETERINARIAN

Once upon a time, there was a girl who loved animals. Karin took care of anything her mother would let her keep in the house: dogs and cats, of course, but also mice, snakes, ducks—even bugs! Some parents wouldn't allow a small zoo in their home, but Karin's parents were very supportive.

Karin had been born in Germany. Before she was five years old, her family moved: first to Canada, then to the United States, where they bounced around from state to state. Karin ran around outdoors, camped, and cared for animals wherever they went. By six years old, Karin knew exactly what she wanted to do when she grew up. She would become a veterinarian.

After she graduated from veterinary school in 1981, Karin was ready for adventure. She packed up her van and drove to Fairbanks, Alaska, to take a job as a vet. She also discovered a popular local sport: dogsledding.

Karin built her own sled out of boards and skis, and got a big Saint Bernard mix to pull it. She loved the feeling of racing across the snow with her dog. For a person who loved being outdoors and being with animals, it was a perfect fit for her. She officially became a dog musher and got a better sled—and more dogs! She volunteered as a race veterinarian, too, caring for dogs as they ran hundreds of miles in cold and icy conditions, making sure they didn't get injured or overworked. Eventually, she became the head veterinarian for the Iditarod, the most famous sled dog race in the world.

SEPTEMBER 16, 1885–DECEMBER 4, 1952
GERMANY ➔ CANADA AND UNITED STATES OF AMERICA

ILLUSTRATION BY
ELENIA BERETTA

"THERE ARE THOSE OF US WHO
REALLY CARE. THERE ARE PEOPLE
SETTING VERY HIGH STANDARDS
FOR DOG CARE."
—KARIN SCHMIDT

KEIKO FUKUDA

JUDOKA

As a girl growing up in Japan, Keiko studied calligraphy, flower arranging, and tea ceremony like other proper young women. One day, she decided she was going to learn **judo**, too.

Keiko was no ordinary student. Her grandfather was a samurai and a jujitsu master, and her judo teacher was one of her grandfather's best students. He had invented this new martial art where opponents use balance and strength to pin each other to the mat. He sent Keiko a special invitation to train with him.

At first, Keiko was shocked to see women judoka—judo athletes—being aggressive and physical. But a person didn't have to be big to succeed at judo. They just had to be smart, strong, and willing to work hard.

When Keiko found out that she would have to give up judo to go through with an arranged marriage, she made a decision. She would not marry. Her fellow judoka would be her family instead.

Before he died, Keiko's teacher asked his students to go teach judo around the world. So that's what Keiko did. She moved to the United States to teach this new sport, and all the while, she rose higher in judo's ranks. By 2006, she was a ninth-degree black belt and the highest-ranking female judoka in the world. Just one step remained to judo's highest rank—a position no woman had ever achieved before.

In 2011, at the age of ninety-eight, Keiko was promoted to tenth-degree black belt by USA Judo. She was the first woman to earn judo's highest honor.

APRIL 12, 1913–FEBRUARY 9, 2013

JAPAN ➔ UNITED STATES OF AMERICA

ILLUSTRATION BY
HELEN LI

"BE STRONG, BE GENTLE,
BE BEAUTIFUL."
—KEIKO FUKUDA

LASKARINA "BOUBOULINA" PINOTSIS

NAVAL COMMANDER

Once upon a time, there was a girl named Laskarina, and she was born to be a rebel. Her father, a Greek sea captain, was thrown in jail for helping to plan a rebellion against the Ottomans, who ruled Greece at the time. Laskarina was born inside a prison within the Ottoman Empire, in a country that is now known as Turkey, during one of her mother's visits to her father. It was the first time she would take people by surprise—but not the last.

After her first husband died, Laskarina married a rich trader who commanded many ships. When he died, too, Laskarina took over his boats and his business, and ordered several new ships of her own. She named the largest one *Agamemnon*, after the king in Greek mythology.

With her fleet of ships, Laskarina joined a secret organization working to end the Ottoman Empire's rule. The organization's only woman, she used her own money to buy weapons and pay soldiers who would fight under her command to free Greece. When the day of the uprising came at last, Laskarina sailed into battle as a commander, directing her ships to go wherever her fellow rebels needed them most.

Under her command, Laskarina's ships stopped supplies from reaching their enemies, and her soldiers captured fortresses and saved Greek towns from destruction. She also saved innocent people from being killed.

Laskarina died in 1825, a few years before her dream of an independent Greece came true.

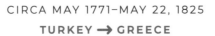

CIRCA MAY 1771–MAY 22, 1825

TURKEY → GREECE

ILLUSTRATION BY
ALICE PIAGGIO

"FORWARD!"
—LASKARINA "BOUBOULINA"
PINOTSIS

LINA BO BARDI

ARCHITECT

Once there was a girl who loved to draw houses, but she didn't want her drawings to stay on paper. She wanted to bring them to life. When Achillina Bo (known as Lina) told her father she wanted to be an architect, he was doubtful. Very few women chose architecture as a career. But Lina went to architecture school anyway.

Lina opened her own architecture studio in Milan when she was twenty-eight. With World War II thundering through Europe, business was slow. Later, her studio was destroyed by bombs and never rebuilt. Eventually, Lina left Italy with her new husband, an art critic named Pietro Maria Bardi. In 1947, Pietro was asked to establish an art museum in São Paulo, Brazil. After they arrived in South America, Lina reopened her studio and designed one of her first Brazilian projects: their house.

Lina called it Casa de Vidro, or "Glass House." It looked like a greenhouse hanging in the rainforest canopy. Casa de Vidro was good practice for Lina's next big project: designing the new home of the São Paulo art museum. The Museu de Arte de São Paulo is also a modern building. It looks like a glass box suspended above the ground, and is considered to be one of Lina's most important works. Perhaps because she was a foreign-born woman, Lina's architectural skill was often overshadowed by Brazilian-born men. But today many consider Lina to be one of the best— and most overlooked—architects of the twentieth century.

DECEMBER 5, 1914–MARCH 20, 1992
ITALY ➡ BRAZIL

ILLUSTRATION BY
ABELLE HAYFORD

"I AM CURIOUS
AND THIS QUALITY
BROADENS MY
HORIZONS."
—LINA BO BARDI

LISA STHALEKAR

CRICKET CHAMPION AND COMMENTATOR

Once upon a time, there was a girl who was adopted by a loving family who supported her dreams. Lisa spent the first three weeks of her life in an orphanage in India. One day, a family came to the orphanage—a man, a woman, and a little girl—and as soon as they saw Lisa, they knew she was meant to be their daughter and sister. They adopted Lisa and brought her home to Michigan.

Lisa's family moved to Kenya before settling in Australia when she was four years old. From the beginning, Lisa took after her father. She shared his love of stamp collecting, classical music, and, most important, his love of cricket. Lisa's father was from India, too, and cricket was the most popular sport in the country.

Growing up, Lisa spent a lot of time playing cricket in the backyard, usually with boys. She didn't know that girls or women played cricket until her father took her to watch a women's match. It wasn't long before Lisa was a professional player herself. By the time she was eighteen, Lisa was playing for the Women's National Cricket League. She later became one of the top women cricketers in Australia, playing for two of the country's World Cup–winning teams.

In 2013, she retired from the sport and became a cricket commentator. She also started using her influence to encourage people to adopt, so other children could have the same opportunities she had. "My story is a really positive one," Lisa said. "Kids deserve to have a permanent, loving, and safe home available to them."

BORN AUGUST 13, 1979

INDIA ➜ UNITED STATES OF AMERICA, KENYA, AND AUSTRALIA

"SPORT HAS SUCH A UNIQUE CAPACITY TO BRING DIFFERENT CULTURES TOGETHER."
—LISA STHALEKAR

ILLUSTRATION BY
KARINA COCQ

LIZ CLAIBORNE

FASHION DESIGNER AND CEO

Anne Elisabeth Claiborne was born in Belgium to American parents. Her father didn't think it was important for her to graduate from school, so Liz took up painting instead. When her family moved to the United States in 1939, she was on her way to becoming a professional artist.

Liz started to dream of being a fashion designer after she sketched a high-collared coat that won a contest. With fifty dollars in her pocket, she moved to New York and got a job as a sketch artist for a women's clothing designer. For the next twenty years or so, she worked behind the scenes in the fashion industry.

But Liz didn't want to be like other fashion designers. Instead of creating glamorous clothing for high-priced boutiques, she wanted to design inexpensive styles for everyday life. Most business clothing for women was a little boring, and Liz thought women should be able to look stylish and professional but still be comfortable.

Liz launched her fashion line in 1976, and by the end of the decade, women were wearing her imaginative designs everywhere. Her affordable mix-and-match fashions flew off the shelves, and soon her company was making millions of dollars a year. It eventually became one of the first companies founded by a woman to make the Fortune 500, an annual list of the most financially successful companies in the United States.

MARCH 31, 1929–JUNE 26, 2007

BELGIUM → UNITED STATES OF AMERICA

"I WANTED TO DRESS BUSY
AND ACTIVE WOMEN LIKE
MYSELF—WOMEN WHO
DRESS IN A RUSH AND WHO
WEREN'T PERFECT."
—LIZ CLAIBORNE

LORELLA PRAELI

ACTIVIST

Once there was a girl who dreamed of becoming an American **citizen** and helping others become citizens, too. Lorella was two years old when she visited the United States for the first time. Back home in Peru, she had been hit by a car and lost one of her legs. Her parents brought her to a special hospital in the US. "My parents were determined that I would reach my full potential and not be limited by my disability," Lorella said.

Lorella and her parents made so many trips to the American hospital that, when she was ten years old, Lorella's family moved to Connecticut. She didn't know that she and her family were **undocumented** immigrants until she filled out college applications. This meant they didn't have the same protection and opportunities as legal citizens. She worried that her family would be forced to leave.

When she was in college, Lorella learned about United We Dream, a network of young people working on behalf of immigrant rights. She met undocumented people who weren't afraid of their status, and it gave her courage. Lorella volunteered with United We Dream, became their director of advocacy and policy, and later worked for political campaigns.

Lorella has devoted her life to immigration reform. Along the way, she's shared her own story and challenged politicians to take action. She became a US citizen in 2015, but her work is not done. "I feel even more committed to continue to fight," Lorella said.

BORN AUGUST 18, 1988
PERU ➡ UNITED STATES OF AMERICA

"I CAN NO LONGER JUST SIT AND WAIT FOR SOMETHING TO HAPPEN."
—LORELLA PRAELI

ILLUSTRATION BY JEANNE DETALLANTE

LUPE GONZALO

MIGRANT FARMER AND LABOR ORGANIZER

Every mile of the long, difficult journey from Guatemala to the United States, Lupe thought of her children back home. She missed them terribly but hoped that the money she would earn as a migrant worker in the United States could give them a better life.

Lupe found work picking fruits and vegetables in Immokalee, Florida. She spent hours in the fields lugging heavy baskets of tomatoes and peppers in temperatures well over a hundred degrees. But even after filling baskets all day, she earned only enough to pay for food and a bed in a crowded trailer.

Worse than the labor was the way she and other women workers were treated. Sometimes employers refused to pay them. Sometimes they touched Lupe and her fellow workers in ways that made them angry, afraid, and uncomfortable. They said ugly things to them and abused them. Lupe knew she and the other workers deserved to be treated with respect. One day, she decided she could be silent no longer.

Lupe joined a group called the Coalition of Immokalee Workers. She helped start a project called the Fair Food Program. This program asked grocery stores and restaurants to buy food only from farms that paid workers fairly and gave them safe and healthy working conditions. Thanks to Lupe and her fellow organizers, some of the biggest food companies in the world have committed to the Fair Food Program, and countless workers' lives are better.

BORN CIRCA 1980

GUATEMALA ➡ UNITED STATES OF AMERICA

"WE ARE HUMAN BEINGS, WE ARE WOMEN, AND NOBODY IS GOING TO KEEP STEPPING ON OUR DIGNITY."
—LUPE GONZALO

ILLUSTRATION BY SALLY CAULWELL

LUPITA AMONDI NYONG'O

Lupita Nyong'o was an adult when she finally had the courage to admit she wanted to be an actor. She had a college degree and an office job, but she left that behind to fly back to Kenya for other opportunities and to plan for her future. Almost six years later, Lupita won her first Oscar.

Lupita's parents had left their home in Kenya for political reasons, so Lupita was born in Mexico and given a Spanish name. Her family returned to Kenya when Lupita was about a year old, but she never forgot the country where she was born. When she was a teenager, Lupita lived in Mexico for a few months to learn Spanish. Today she has both Kenyan and Mexican citizenship and speaks four languages: Luo, Spanish, English, and Swahili.

Lupita was a star from the start of her career as an actor. She was nominated for a Golden Globe and won an Oscar for her first major role. She has starred in many more movies since then.

But not all of Lupita's work happens in Hollywood. She also uses her influence to bring attention to issues that are close to her heart. She has even written a children's book about a young Kenyan girl named Sulwe, who has the darkest skin in her family. Like Lupita herself, Sulwe learns to see her own beauty and accept herself for who she is.

BORN MARCH 1, 1983

MEXICO → KENYA AND UNITED STATES OF AMERICA

ILLUSTRATION BY
MONICA AHANONU

"NO MATTER WHERE YOU'RE FROM,
YOUR DREAMS ARE VALID."
—LUPITA AMONDI NYONG'O

MADELEINE ALBRIGHT

POLITICIAN

When she was a little girl, Madeleine's family fled their home in Czechoslovakia, which is now known as the Czech Republic. Her parents said they left for political reasons. But more than fifty years later, Madeleine learned the truth: her family was Jewish. They left the country and became Catholic to be safe from the Nazis. After World War II, her family returned, but they didn't stay long. In 1948, eleven-year-old Madeleine crossed the Atlantic on a huge ship to start a new life in America.

In Europe, Madeleine's father had been a **diplomat**. In the United States, he taught political science at a university. Madeleine shared her father's enthusiasm for politics and global issues. After marrying Joseph Albright and having three daughters, Madeleine earned her PhD in public law and government.

After working in politics for many years, Madeleine became the first woman to ever be US secretary of state. She was a foreign policy expert and a champion for human rights. But she also became known for something surprising: her pin collection. Madeleine often wore pins—a coiled snake, an eagle, a heart—to communicate her thoughts without words. The pins were a way to start conversation or make people smile. When asked about her favorite diplomatic accessory, Madeleine said: "In order to get through a lot of complicated issues, it helps to have a little bit of humor."

BORN MAY 15, 1937
CZECH REPUBLIC → UNITED STATES OF AMERICA

ILLUSTRATION BY
BARBARA DZIADOSZ

"IT TOOK ME QUITE A LONG
TIME TO DEVELOP A VOICE,
AND NOW THAT I HAVE IT,
I AM NOT GOING TO BE SILENT."
—MADELEINE ALBRIGHT

MALIKA OUFKIR

AUTHOR

O nce there was a girl who lived like royalty. Malika's father was an adviser to King Hassan II of Morocco, and she spent much of her childhood roaming the vast halls of the king's palaces.

Unfortunately, Malika's fairy-tale life was disrupted when her father tried to overthrow the king. As punishment, the king had her father killed and ordered nineteen-year-old Malika, her five brothers and sisters, and her mother thrown into a secret prison in the desert.

For fourteen years, Malika was held in isolated prisons with little food and terrible conditions. When she and her family members were kept apart from one another, one of Malika's brothers managed to set up a secret network between the cells so they could still hear one another speak. When the guards were not listening, Malika entertained her family with stories she had invented to keep their strength and spirits up.

Then came her daring escape. Though she was weak from lack of food, she and two of her siblings managed to dig a secret tunnel with makeshift tools including a spoon and the lid of a sardine can. Malika was worried they'd get caught but even more scared to stay in that prison any longer. When the moment was right, they crawled through the tunnel and ran toward freedom.

Eventually, Malika moved to France and wrote the story of what happened to her family. Because she spoke up about their experience, readers all over the world came to understand what political prisoners endured in Morocco—and the strength it took for them to survive.

BORN APRIL 2, 1953

MOROCCO ➞ FRANCE

"HOWEVER POWERFUL HE WAS,
HOWEVER UNTOUCHABLE HE WAS...
ONE WOMAN WITH NO WEAPONS,
NO POWER, NOTHING, SUCCEEDED
IN DEFEATING HIM."
—MALIKA OUFKIR

MARCELA CONTRERAS

HEMATOLOGIST

Once upon a time, a young woman named Marcela knew she wanted to be a doctor, just like her father was. She began her studies at the University of Chile, where she became interested in something everyone on earth has in common: blood.

Marcela graduated with honors after studying hematology, which is the study of blood, and immunology, which is the study of how bodies defend themselves from illness.

In 1972, Marcela won a scholarship to study and work in the United Kingdom. People were worried about the instability of the government in Chile, so Marcela and her husband decided to move to London with their two children.

At the time, the blood centers in the UK weren't connected to one another, making it hard to send spare donations where they were needed. If the UK had one system for the whole country, it would save countless lives. Marcela was asked to take charge of this special project.

Marcela's leadership made sure that donated blood was always available to people who needed it after surgery, illness, or accidents, no matter where they lived.

Based on the success of this system in the UK, Marcela went on to direct an organization that worked to make sure there was a sufficient supply of safe blood in countries around the world—including her native Chile.

BORN JANUARY 4, 1942

CHILE ➡ UNITED KINGDOM

"EVERYTHING IS POSSIBLE
IN THIS LIFE. IT'S ALL A MATTER
OF HARD WORK AND DETERMINATION.
YOU SHOULD NEVER FEEL LESS
THAN ANYONE BECAUSE YOU'RE
SO FAR AWAY IN THE WORLD."
—MARCELA CONTRERAS

MARIA GOEPPERT MAYER

THEORETICAL PHYSICIST

Maria was destined to become a professor—just like her father, and his father, grandfather, and so on, for many generations! But because Maria's **ancestors** were men, her path would be a little different.

Maria's specialty was physics. She married an American physicist named Joseph and moved to the United States when Joseph got a job at Johns Hopkins University. But even though Maria was also qualified, the university refused to hire her as professor. It was the Great Depression, a time when there were very few jobs to be had in the US, and people thought that men deserved jobs more than women did.

Maria wasn't about to give up her work. She did her research in an empty office on campus, publishing papers and a scientific book without a paycheck or a title. She did the same thing at Columbia University when Joseph got a job there. And when he found a job at the University of Chicago, the school said Maria could work as a professor, too—as long as they didn't have to pay her!

All the while, Maria continued her important work in science, including nuclear physics. With her research partners, she figured out why some atoms were more stable than others. This was a breakthrough—a big one. In 1963, Maria won the Nobel Prize for her discoveries. She was the second woman, after Marie Curie, to win the prize in physics.

JUNE 28, 1906–FEBRUARY 20, 1972

POLAND → UNITED STATES OF AMERICA

"WINNING THE PRIZE WASN'T HALF AS EXCITING AS DOING THE WORK ITSELF."
—MARIA GOEPPERT MAYER

ILLUSTRATION BY ANNALISA VENTURA

MARJANE SATRAPI

GRAPHIC NOVELIST

Once there was a girl who used her art to stand up against an unjust government. When Marjane was young, big changes happened in Iran. It started with a **revolution** and a war with Iraq. At first, some people thought the revolution might be a good thing. There were big celebrations in the streets the day it happened.

Marjane and her parents were Muslim like the new government leaders were, but they disagreed with their politics. After the revolution, Iran had a strict religious government. Each time the government created a new rule, Marjane would bend it. When it said all women must wear veils, Marjane let her hair show. When it created a dress code, she wore forbidden sneakers and a denim jacket. When certain music was banned, she secretly bought cassette tapes of it. And when her teachers praised Iran's leaders, she asked brave questions.

Marjane's parents were proud of their daughter, but they were scared, too. She could go to jail for her behavior. Her parents eventually sent her to boarding school in Austria, where she'd be safer.

After high school, Marjane moved to France to study art. She had always loved comics, so she created some of her own. Using simple black-and-white drawings, she told the story of her childhood in Iran. A publisher bought her graphic novel, *Persepolis*, and it became an international best seller. Later, Marjane helped turn the book into an Oscar-nominated film. Since settling in France, Marjane continues to use art to tell stories about the home she left behind.

BORN NOVEMBER 22, 1969

IRAN ➡ FRANCE

"ONE ISN'T BORN COURAGEOUS.
ONE BECOMES IT."
—MARJANE SATRAPI

ILLUSTRATION BY
ELENA DE SANTI

MARTA EMPINOTTI

BASE JUMPER

Once there was a girl who dreamed of flying. The first time Marta went skydiving, she was only a teenager. She fell in love with the feeling of weightlessness, of soaring above the world like a bird.

Her family taught her to always be independent and never be tied down. Marta loved her parents and three sisters in Brazil, but there was so much of the world to see. She went traveling, and her first stop was the United States, where there was lots of skydiving, and something else exciting, too: BASE jumping. She decided to make the US her new home.

Instead of leaping from a plane, BASE jumpers use their parachutes to leap from places high above the earth, like bridges, cliffs, or tall buildings. It can be very dangerous, but Marta always made sure to be professionally strapped into her parachute. Marta loved the feeling of jumping better than anything else in the world.

Marta has made more than sixteen hundred jumps and is one of the sport's most respected athletes. She has traveled all over the world in search of new adventures, and has jumped from skyscrapers in Malaysia, waterfalls in Venezuela, and many places in between. BASE jumping has enabled her to see the world in a whole new way.

"When I'm high above the ground, maybe six or eight hundred feet up, the feeling is very spiritual," Marta said. "On the horizon, the sun is rising, turning the clouds pink and yellow. It's so peaceful; it's like paradise.... It's just me and nature. Then I jump and feel the thrill. When I land, I see the sunrise again. How many people watch the sunrise twice in one day?"

BORN DECEMBER 18, 1964

BRAZIL ➜ UNITED STATES OF AMERICA

"YOU NEED TO CHOOSE WHAT MAKES YOU HAPPY, AND THIS DECISION MIGHT NOT BE THE EASIEST, BUT IT IS DEFINITELY THE RIGHT ONE."
—MARTA EMPINOTTI

ILLUSTRATION BY SARAH LOULENDO

MERLENE JOYCE OTTEY

SPRINTER

Once there was a girl who could run like the wind. Her name was Merlene. Merlene lived in Jamaica and ran everywhere she could. Her family did not have much money, and she often had to race barefoot when she and her schoolmates competed against one another. She still ran faster than almost everyone else. Sometimes when she crossed the finish line, she was surprised to see how many runners were still on the track trying to finish the race!

When Merlene was sixteen years old, she heard that a Jamaican man had won the gold medal in the men's 200-meter dash at the Olympic Games, and she wondered how far racing could take her, too.

Four years later, it was Merlene's turn in Moscow, Russia. She took home the bronze medal in the women's 200-meter dash—the first Olympic medal ever won by a Caribbean woman.

Merlene competed in the Olympics six times after that—more than any other track-and-field athlete—and won eight more Olympic medals.

At an age when many runners retire, Merlene moved to Slovenia and decided to compete for her new home country. In 2004, she ran in her seventh Olympics, advancing to the semifinals over runners half her age.

In 2014, Merlene moved again—this time to Switzerland. She still holds the world record for the women's indoor 200-meter sprint.

BORN MAY 10, 1960

JAMAICA ➜ SLOVENIA AND SWITZERLAND

ILLUSTRATION BY
LUISA RIVERA

531

"I JUST LOVE RUNNING.
ONCE YOU LOVE SOMETHING,
YOU CAN PUT UP WITH ALL
THE TORTURE."
—MERLENE JOYCE OTTEY

MIN JIN LEE

AUTHOR

Min looked nervously around her classroom in New York City. It was 1976, and seven-year-old Min had just moved from South Korea with her sisters and parents. All around her, children chatted away in English, a language Min did not know. When she tried to say new words, classmates laughed at her. Being laughed at hurt, so she didn't speak often.

As a teenager, Min traveled two hours each way by train to her high school. Though the trip was long, Min never felt alone. She loved to read, and she always brought a book with her on her journeys. As the trains rumbled across bridges and under streets throughout New York City, she lost herself in new worlds and characters.

Min went to law school and became a lawyer, but she never stopped believing in the power of storytelling. She wanted to become a writer and tell stories that she understood from her own life and those of the people around her—people who had moved away from their first countries and settled all around the world, carving new lives for themselves in societies that often ignored or belittled their experiences.

Min's first novel, *Free Food for Millionaires*, was published in 2007. She then moved to Tokyo for four years to write the epic story of a Korean family living in Japan—it was called *Pachinko*. When *Pachinko* was published in 2017, it earned recognition as a National Book Award finalist, a number of other honors, and the admiration of readers all over the world who fell in love with the stories and characters Min created.

BORN NOVEMBER 11, 1968

SOUTH KOREA ➔ UNITED STATES OF AMERICA

ILLUSTRATION BY
EVA RUST

"MY FAMILY NEVER WENT
ANYWHERE. BUT I'D READ SO
MANY NOVELS THAT, IN MY MIND,
I'D SORT OF BEEN EVERYWHERE."
—MIN JIN LEE

MIN MEHTA

ORTHOPEDIC SURGEON

Sit up straight! When she was eleven, Min heard that from more adults than she could count. Then one day, a family friend who was also a nurse said something that changed her life. She revealed that Min couldn't sit up straight because she had scoliosis—a curve in her spine.

Although she was born in Iran, Min grew up in India in the 1930s, when there wasn't much that doctors could do to help children with scoliosis. Min wanted to change that. She had known since she was six years old that she wanted to be a doctor when she grew up. By the time she finished medical school in India, she knew exactly what kind of doctor she wanted to be: a surgeon.

Min decided to move to the UK to continue her medical training. There were hardly any women working as surgeons at that time, so when Min was offered an interview in London, the other doctors were shocked when she walked in the room—they had thought *Min* was a man's name!

Min became one of the most respected **orthopedic** surgeons in the UK for her study of scoliosis in children. She realized that in many cases, if a child's back could be held in the correct position for enough time, starting when they were very small, the extra curve in their spine would straighten naturally as the child grew. Min taught other surgeons how to use a special plaster cast, now called a Mehta cast, to correct children's spines without surgery.

Doctors today still use Mehta casts to treat scoliosis in children.

NOVEMBER 1, 1926–AUGUST 23, 2017
IRAN ➡ INDIA AND UNITED KINGDOM

ILLUSTRATION BY
MEEL TAMPHANON

"LIKE WILDFLOWERS...
SOME CAN WITHSTAND
MOTHER NATURE'S
ELEMENTS AND GROW
STRAIGHT, WHILE OTHERS
NEED A LITTLE GUIDANCE
IN THE BEGINNING."
—MIN MEHTA

MUZOON ALMELLEHAN

ACTIVIST

Once there was a girl who loved learning so much, not even a war could stop her from getting an education. Muzoon lived a comfortable, happy life in Syria. She was surrounded by a loving family and friendly neighbors. And she was a dedicated student who dreamed of traveling the world as a journalist.

But when Muzoon was eleven years old, a war overtook her country, and her parents were forced to leave Syria. Muzoon could pack just one bag, and she filled it with her most prized possessions: her schoolbooks. Her father told her to pack less, but Muzoon insisted, "These books are my power. These books are my future."

Muzoon and her family lived in a **refugee** camp for the next few years, sharing a single tent with no electricity. The camp had schools, but Muzoon discovered that many children—especially girls—didn't attend. She walked through the camp, encouraging parents to send their daughters to school.

In 2015, Muzoon and her family finally settled in England. Their new home welcomed them, and she made many friends. But Muzoon couldn't forget her fellow refugees. In 2017, she became a Goodwill Ambassador for UNICEF, the youngest person to ever be chosen for the role at the time. At university, Muzoon continues to campaign for girls' education. And her homeland has never been far from her heart. "I believe in the Syrian people, especially in the Syrian children," she said. "I believe we are strong enough to rebuild our country."

BORN CIRCA APRIL 1998

SYRIA → ENGLAND

"IN THE MIDDLE OF THE DARKNESS, LEARNING GIVES YOU LIGHT."
—MUZOON ALMELLEHAN

ILLUSTRATION BY MALIHA ABIDI

NADINE BURKE HARRIS

PEDIATRICIAN

Once there was a girl who wanted to be a pediatrician so she could help children be healthy. With a father who was a scientist and a mother who was a nurse, Nadine knew from an early age how science could help people.

After moving from Jamaica to California as a kid, Nadine often felt out of place because there were few immigrants or children of color in her school. At first, she spoke English using a Jamaican dialect called patois. This made it difficult for classmates and teachers to understand her. But these challenges didn't stop Nadine from excelling in school.

Nadine studied medicine for a long time and eventually became a pediatrician. She opened a pediatric clinic in one of the poorest and most underserved neighborhoods in San Francisco. Over time, Nadine noticed that her most unhealthy patients had something in common: they had a lot of stress and difficulties in their lives. Rather than simply treating her young patients' symptoms, Nadine wanted to treat the cause. She created an organization to research childhood trauma. "I was inspired to make sure that every child has an equal opportunity to grow up healthy," Nadine said.

In 2019, Nadine was asked to be California's first-ever surgeon general—the head of public health policy and spokesperson for medical issues. In her new role, Nadine continued to help children who have experienced toxic stress. According to Nadine, the sooner doctors understand their patients' problems, the sooner their patients can be healed.

BORN OCTOBER 9, 1975
JAMAICA ➔ UNITED STATES OF AMERICA

ILLUSTRATION BY
VERONICA CARRATELLO

"I'D RATHER FAIL TRYING
TO DO SOMETHING GOOD
IN THE WORLD THAN
SUCCEED AT DOING NOTHING."
—NADINE BURKE HARRIS

NAMI AND REN HAYAKAWA

ARCHERS

Nami stood still and strong as a statue, the string of her bow pulled tight. With a sound like a whisper, she let go. Her arrow shot through the air and plunged straight into the center of the target. Another bull's-eye.

Nami wasn't the only girl from South Korea who loved archery. Every four years, the country watched spellbound as the South Korean national team—the finest in the world—competed in the Olympics, taking most of the gold medals home with them.

Nami's sister, Ren, also took up archery after watching Nami practice the sport. Both girls eventually followed their mother to Japan, where she'd moved several years earlier.

In 2008, Nami competed in archery in the Beijing Olympics for Japan, but lost in the quarterfinal. Ren went to college in Japan on an archery scholarship but didn't think she was strong enough to compete in the Olympics. Nami encouraged her to try anyway. At the trials, Ren didn't just do well—she earned a spot on the team!

At the 2012 Olympics in London, a reporter asked Ren what her goal for the competition was. "I want to give everything I have so that after it's all over, I can look back on it and become satisfied with myself," she said. And that's what she did. Together with her teammates, Ren earned a bronze medal in the team competition, the first women's archery medal brought home to Japan.

NAMI, BORN NOVEMBER 6, 1984 • REN, BORN AUGUST 24, 1987
SOUTH KOREA ➔ JAPAN

ILLUSTRATION BY
YASMINE GATEAU

"SINCE WE WON A MEDAL
AT THE OLYMPIC GAMES,
I HOPE THIS WILL HELP MAKE
ARCHERY MORE POPULAR
IN JAPAN AMONG CHILDREN."
—REN HAYAKAWA

NIKI YANG

ANIMATOR AND VOICE ACTOR

Once there was a girl who wanted to share her wild imagination with the world. Niki grew up in South Korea, where she went to school, practiced the violin, and learned to run a household. The first time Niki picked up a comic book, however, she discovered a new world. The colorful illustrations and stories fascinated her. One day she decided she wanted to create characters and worlds of her own.

Niki's traditional family had other plans. Her mother wanted Niki to marry a doctor or lawyer. No one expected a young woman like her to pursue a career of her own. But that's exactly what she did. Niki eventually moved to the US to study animation at the California Institute of the Arts. Then she worked at a few animation studios and became a storyboard artist and writer. The animated shows she helped create became very popular and opened new doors for Niki's career.

One of Niki's biggest challenges during her first years in America was learning to speak English. But her accent and ability to speak Korean led to a surprising opportunity. One of her friends was creating an animated series called *Adventure Time* and needed a voice actor who spoke Korean. Niki auditioned for the part and was hired! Shortly afterward, she was also hired for an English-speaking part on the show.

Niki has continued to work as an animator and voice actor, and to branch out into new areas of filmmaking. After years of working on other successful shows, Niki even started developing a pilot for her own animated series.

BORN SEPTEMBER 19, 1982
SOUTH KOREA → UNITED STATES OF AMERICA

"DON'T FORGET TO HAVE FUN WITH WHAT YOU DO! THAT'S WHERE TRUE CREATIVITY COMES FROM."
—NIKI YANG

ILLUSTRATION BY
DECUE WU

NOOR INAYAT KHAN

SPY

Once upon a time, there was a girl named Noor whose mother was an American poet and whose father was a musician and Indian prince who believed in tolerance and nonviolence. Her family moved frequently, from Moscow to London to Paris, until her father died unexpectedly. Although Noor was only thirteen, she took care of her brothers, her sister, and her heartbroken mother.

When World War II began in Europe, Noor fled with her family to England, where she became a radio operator. Because she could speak French, the British government chose Noor to join a special group of spies in France sending secret wireless messages between British and French agents. Some of her bosses weren't sure if she could handle the job because of her childlike nature. Beneath her gentle exterior, though, was a brave spirit.

As a spy, Noor pretended to be a children's nurse named Jeanne-Marie. In reality, she was one of the sharpest and most skilled radio operators in the **resistance**. When other agents in her network were found out and arrested, Noor took over their tasks, until she was doing the work of six operators at once.

Eventually, Noor was captured and killed by the Nazis. Her last word was *"liberté"*—freedom. Noor was awarded the George Cross and the French Croix de Guerre after her death, the highest award for bravery outside of combat.

JANUARY 1, 1914–SEPTEMBER 13, 1944

RUSSIA ➜ ENGLAND AND FRANCE

"THE PATH OF THE HEART IS THORNY, / WHICH LEADS IN THE END TO BLISS."
—NOOR INAYAT KHAN

ILLUSTRATION BY
YEVHENIA HAIDAMAKA

OLGA KORBUT

GYMNAST

Once there was a girl who went from being an unknown teenager to a gymnastics superstar seemingly overnight. When Olga was in second grade, a coach visited her classroom and asked if anyone was interested in gymnastics. The sport reminded her of acrobatics at the circus, and Olga was excited to learn more.

After her first few lessons, Olga began to train more formally. By 1972, she earned a spot on the Soviet Union's Olympic team! She was one of the youngest and smallest members, but at the Summer Games in Munich, Olga surprised everyone.

Gymnasts were usually known for their elegance, but Olga was a different kind of gymnast. She wowed the judges with technical skills and acrobatics that had never been seen before. A new kind of backflip was later named after her: the Korbut flip. Olga also freely showed her emotions. She cried after her mistakes and grinned when she did well. Her fearlessness and spunky personality made her a fan favorite.

At her first Olympics, Olga won four medals—three gold and one silver. Around the world, girls signed up for gymnastics and wrote letters to their new hero. Olga received so much fan mail—twenty thousand letters a year—that her hometown hired a postal worker just for her. In 1988, she was the first person to be inducted into the International Gymnastics Hall of Fame. A few years later, Olga moved to the United States, where she still teaches gymnastics to young athletes today.

BORN MAY 16, 1955

BELARUS → UNITED STATES OF AMERICA

"I WAS BORN TO DO
GYMNASTICS."
—OLGA KORBUT

PAULA NEWBY-FRASER

TRIATHLETE

Once there was a girl who was good at swimming and running. Paula was born in Zimbabwe and moved with her family to South Africa when she was four years old. When Paula was twenty-two, she heard about an upcoming local triathlon: a race where competitors have to swim, cycle, and run.

Paula knew she could do two of those sports, but she had never tried cycling before. Still, she bought a bike, entered the race—and won the women's event! Shortly after, she became the women's triathlon champion in South Africa. She decided to train as a professional triathlete and moved to the United States.

The biggest triathlon of all was the Ironman World Championship, held in Kona, Hawaii. Competitors had to swim for 2.4 miles, bike for 112 miles, and run 26.2 miles, one right after the other.

Paula entered the race in 1986 and was the first woman to ever finish in under ten hours. In 1988, she smashed the women's course record. She won five of the next six Ironman World Championships. People called her the Queen of Kona. Then in 1995, with less than a mile to go in the race, her body broke down. She finished fourth, feeling sad and disappointed. She decided she would do the race again, but this time she would train a different way than her competitors did—and she would run just for her own enjoyment. She did it—and won her eighth Ironman!

Paula has more Ironman championship wins than any triathlete ever. The world record time she set in 1992 stood for seventeen years.

BORN JUNE 2, 1962

ZIMBABWE ➔ SOUTH AFRICA AND UNITED STATES OF AMERICA

ILLUSTRATION BY
JEANNE DETALLANTE

"TO ME THE GREATEST
LESSON AS AN ATHLETE
AND IN TRAINING IS
JUST DON'T GET GREEDY
KNOW THAT YOU HAVE
TO GET UP AND GO AGAIN
THE NEXT DAY."
—PAULA NEWBY-FRASER

PEARL TRAN AND THU GETKA

DENTISTS

Thu was seventeen and Pearl just twelve when their lives changed forever. A war between their country, South Vietnam, and neighboring North Vietnam was coming to a close. Many people, Thu's and Pearl's families included, chose to flee rather than risk violence at home.

Both of their families moved to the United States. Thu's family settled in Virginia, Pearl's in Georgia. There, they began new lives.

Though they didn't know each other, Thu's and Pearl's careers began to follow surprisingly similar paths. Both were good students who excelled in science and biology. Thu went to dental school, and Pearl—after first trying medical school, where she couldn't stand the long hours—did the same. They even became the same kind of dentist: a periodontist, who specializes in caring for people's gums.

Pearl eventually decided to become a dentist for the US Navy. She was assigned to a residency at the National Naval Medical Center in Bethesda, Maryland. Shortly after her arrival, a new periodontist came to the center to be Pearl's mentor. It was Thu! She had also joined the US Navy. In fact, she was the first Vietnamese American woman to be promoted to the rank of colonel in the US Navy.

The two women were stunned to realize how similar their lives had been. Leaving their homes in Vietnam and becoming refugees had been a scary experience, but Pearl and Thu both built new lives and went on to use their talents to serve the country they adopted as their own.

PEARL TRAN, BORN CIRCA 1963 • THU GETKA, BORN CIRCA 1958

VIETNAM ➔ UNITED STATES OF AMERICA

"AS A KID IN SAIGON, I DIDN'T UNDERSTAND A LOT OF THINGS THAT WERE GOING ON BEFORE I LEFT VIETNAM."
—PEARL TRAN

ILLUSTRATION BY
VALENCIA SPATES

PNINA TAMANO-SHATA

LAWYER AND LAWMAKER

Once there was a Jewish girl named Pnina who was born in Ethiopia. The government made it hard for people like Pnina's family to practice their religion, and during a time of civil war and famine, they fled to a **refugee** camp in Sudan before immigrating to Israel.

Even though Pnina had lived in Israel since she was three years old, she was given a hard time by other children at school. Her parents found jobs as cleaners and worked hard to provide for her and her siblings, but because they didn't speak Hebrew, Pnina had to speak for them at school, the doctor's, and the social work office. She understood how hard life was for people who were different and who did not have a voice.

When she got to college, Pnina led protests against **racism**, her voice carrying clear and strong. After graduating, she went to work as a television journalist. When her bosses asked her to cover a protest of Ethiopian Israelis, Pnina realized that she could not simply stand to the side. She put down her microphone and joined the **protesters** herself!

Pnina decided to become a lawyer and fight against **discrimination**. In 2013, she became a member of the Knesset, Israel's parliament—the first Ethiopian-born woman to represent her community there.

"My experiences growing up as an Ethiopian in Israel had prepared me well to help others, too," she said. "I felt like I had a responsibility toward Israeli society to make things better."

BORN NOVEMBER 1, 1981
ETHIOPIA ➜ ISRAEL

ILLUSTRATION BY OLIVIA FIELDS

"WE NEED TO SPEAK LOUDLY AND WORK HARD. BUT NEVER FORGET WHERE WE CAME FROM."
—PNINA TAMANO-SHATA

RAPELANG RABANA

COMPUTER SCIENTIST AND ENTREPRENEUR

Once there was a girl who wanted an education more than anything. But when she was a teenager, Rapelang worried she wouldn't be able to take her final high school exams.

Rapelang's family had moved to South Africa from nearby Botswana. Her parents worked hard to send her to boarding school, but it was expensive. If they couldn't pay, Rapelang couldn't continue her studies. Faced with a tricky problem, Rapelang earned a scholarship for her final term—and passed her exams with honors.

Rapelang then went to the University of Cape Town in South Africa and studied computer science. She liked how coding let her create new things from her own imagination. When she graduated, she knew she didn't want to go work for a big business that would tell her what to do all day. She wanted to go her own way.

Before most smartphones existed, Rapelang and a friend started a company called Yeigo that let people speak over the internet, instead of over expensive phone lines. Their company was a huge success as it made that personal connection more affordable.

For her next big project, Rapelang returned to her love of education. She started an online business called Rekindle Learning to help people of all ages do better in school and work, wherever they lived.

Rapelang is one of the world's most exciting young entrepreneurs. "The opportunities to be whoever you want to be have never been more accessible to those who pursue their dreams," she said.

BORN NOVEMBER 5, 1983

BOTSWANA → SOUTH AFRICA AND UNITED STATES OF AMERICA

"TRUE SUCCESS COMES FROM OPERATING FROM AN AUTHENTIC SPACE AND BEING TRUE TO YOUR OWN GOALS AND ASPIRATIONS."
—RAPELANG RABANA

ILLUSTRATION BY MICHELLE D'URBANO

REYNA DUONG

. . . .

CHEF

Once there was a girl who believed all people should be treated with respect, no matter their abilities. Before Reyna turned three, her family left Vietnam as refugees and moved to the United States, where her little brother, Sang, was born.

Sang was born with Down syndrome, and Reyna did her best to look out for him. Their childhood was not easy, but Reyna's happiest times were helping her mother in the kitchen. Her mother made meals from scratch, including broth, which took two whole days.

When their parents passed away, Reyna became Sang's guardian. To help her and her brother feel less sad, Reyna cooked familiar meals that reminded them of their mother. The experience inspired Reyna to open a sandwich shop in their mother's honor.

Reyna filled the menu with delicious banh mi, but sharing good food wasn't her only purpose. Reyna wanted to run a business where she and Sang could work together. She wanted to show her community that people with Down syndrome deserve the opportunity to work just like everyone else.

Today Sang and many other people with differing abilities work in Reyna's restaurant. And once a year, on World Down Syndrome Day, the restaurant throws a big party. For Reyna, it's a celebration of the brother she loves and the hope she has for a more welcoming world.

. . . .

BORN MAY 30, 1977

VIETNAM → UNITED STATES OF AMERICA

ILLUSTRATION BY
STEPHANIE SINGLETON

"BONDING OVER A MEAL TOGETHER
IS A UNIVERSAL LANGUAGE."
—REYNA DUONG

RIHANNA

Once there was a girl who wanted her music to be heard all over the world. When Rihanna was a teenager, she auditioned for a record label. The producers were so impressed, they encouraged Rihanna to move to the United States. Even though she loved Barbados and her family, she wasn't afraid to leave it all behind. "I wanted to do what I had to do, even if it meant moving to America," Rihanna said.

Not long after she arrived in the US, the label offered her a contract, and her career took off. Her songs played on the radio and fans lined up to see her onstage. Yet it took a while for Rihanna to find her true voice. In Barbadian **culture**, Rihanna said, being quiet was considered polite. But in the US, her quietness was seen as rude. "You mean well, and it can come across in a different way in a different culture," Rihanna said.

Rihanna has built a reputation as an artist and entrepreneur who's true to herself. She's won nine Grammys and is one of the best-selling music artists of all time. Her musical success also opened doors into areas she never expected, including business. In 2017, Rihanna launched Fenty Beauty, a cosmetics brand that focused on inclusivity. She and her team spent two years developing foundation that came in a huge variety of skin tones—more than forty shades. Her company's emphasis on diversity has inspired other cosmetics brands to do the same. Then in 2019, Rihanna created her own luxury fashion line. "The thing that keeps me alive and passionate is being creative," Rihanna said.

BORN FEBRUARY 20, 1988
BARBADOS ➔ UNITED STATES OF AMERICA

"MUSIC HAD LED ME
TO THESE OTHER
OUTLETS, AND
TO THINGS
I GENUINELY LOVE."
—RIHANNA

ILLUSTRATION BY
JESTENIA SOUTHERLAND

ROJA MAYA LIMBU AND SUJANA RANA

UNION ORGANIZERS

Roja was around nineteen years old when she left her home in Nepal and moved to Lebanon. She had trained to be a teacher, but she wanted a better life for herself and was ready to work hard to get it. Eventually she found a job helping an elderly lady in her home, and for more than four years, she worked every single day with no time off.

After several years in Lebanon, Roja met Sujana, who was also from Nepal. Sujana, too, worked long, hard hours as a domestic worker with few rights. Sujana and Roja had sometimes felt isolated and afraid in their jobs. Together, they realized they were not alone.

There were more than 250,000 immigrants in Lebanon who worked as housekeepers, nannies, and caregivers. Some of them were abused by the people they worked for. Sometimes their bosses stole their money or refused time off and kept them confined.

Sujana and Roja wanted to change things for workers like themselves, so along with the others, they decided to form a union.

There were laws to protect workers in Lebanon, but those laws didn't apply to migrant workers like Sujana and Roja, and the government did not approve of the union. In 2016, both Sujana and Roja were arrested and forced to leave Lebanon and return to Nepal. But the work they started continues. Today people in Lebanon are still fighting for fair treatment for domestic workers.

ROJA, BORN AUGUST 6, 1985 • SUJANA, BORN SEPTEMBER 9, 1971

NEPAL ➞ LEBANON

"THEY SAID THAT MY CRIME WAS HELPING THE VICTIM GIRLS.... I HAD DONE THAT, AND IF IT WAS A CRIME, THEN THERE COULD BE NOTHING BETTER THAN THAT."
—SUJANA RANA

ILLUSTRATION BY
ALINE ZALKO

ROSALIE ABELLA

JUDGE

Once upon a time, there was a girl named Rosalie who knew how important it was for laws to treat everyone with the same respect. Her parents were Polish Jewish people who had survived World War II, and Rosalie was born in a **displaced persons** camp.

Rosalie's family moved to Canada when she was small, and although her father had been a lawyer in Germany, he was not allowed to practice law in Canada because he was not a **citizen**.

Only four years after Rosalie became a lawyer herself, she was asked to serve as a judge in Canada's family court. She was the first Jewish woman to become a judge in Canada and one of the youngest judges in the country's history. She was also the first person in Canada to become a judge while pregnant!

Every day she saw people struggling in a system that treated them unfairly because of their gender, disability, or skin color. Rosalie tried her best to listen with an open mind and be fair in her decisions.

"I learned to see law from the experiences of the people who were before me...," Rosalie said later. "Looking at the law and justice from their eyes taught me how to be a judge."

Around 1984, Rosalie was put in charge of a huge job: to figure out how to make workplaces in Canada more equal to all workers. Her report was used in other countries to make their workplaces fairer, too.

In 2004, Rosalie became the first Jewish woman to serve on Canada's Supreme Court.

BORN JULY 1, 1946

GERMANY ➡ CANADA

ILLUSTRATION BY
SASHA KOLESNIK

"WHEN YOU ARE AN
IMMIGRANT, YOU NEVER
THINK IN TERMS
OF ENTITLEMENT.
YOU THINK IN TERMS
OF OPPORTUNITIES
AND WORKING
REALLY HARD."
—ROSALIE ABELLA

ROSE FORTUNE

ENTREPRENEUR AND POLICE OFFICER

Once upon a time, the waterfront in the town of Annapolis Royal, Canada, was a busy place. There were boxes and parcels everywhere, and travelers, sailors, and fishermen came and went at all hours of the night. Some people looked at the waterfront and saw chaos. Rose saw opportunity.

Rose's parents were enslaved when she was born, but they wanted their daughter to grow up free. During the American Revolution, British forces promised Rose's father that he and his family would be freed from slavery if he fought on their side and won. When the American rebels triumphed, Rose's family and many other black families who had sided with the British left the United States and moved to Canada.

Eventually, Rose looked for ways to earn a living at the waterfront.

Using wheelbarrows, she started a business carrying luggage and goods to and from the ships—a business that her family went on to run for more than a hundred years. Rose would even go directly to the inn where her customers were staying and make sure they didn't miss their ship. In the days before alarm clocks or telephones, this was very helpful!

Rose knew everyone on the docks, and she made sure that people obeyed its rules. Wearing heavy boots and a man's coat over her dress and apron, Rose patrolled the waterfront on foot and sent troublemakers running.

She is now recognized as Canada's first female police officer.

MARCH 13, 1774–FEBRUARY 20, 1864
UNITED STATES OF AMERICA ➜ CANADA

ILLUSTRATION BY
SABRENA KHADIJA

ROSELI OCAMPO-FRIEDMANN

MICROBIOLOGIST

Once there was a girl growing up in the Philippines who was fascinated by plants that lived in odd places: moss growing on the sides of buildings, flowers blooming on balconies, tiny weeds curling up through cracks in the sidewalk. Her name was Roseli, and when she went to college at the University of the Philippines, she got a degree in botany, the study of plants.

To continue her education, Roseli moved to Israel to get a graduate degree from Hebrew University. There, she met a scientist named Imre Friedmann. Imre had discovered tiny blue-green algae inside and on the underside of rocks. They mostly grew in deserts or hard-to-reach places, so they were very hard to study. But Roseli was able to grow them in the laboratory. People joked that she had a "blue-green" thumb!

Roseli and Imre got married, settled in the United States, and traveled the world seeking out life-forms that grew in places too cold, hot, dry, or unusual for most other plants. Together, they discovered extremely small living microorganisms within rocks in Antarctica's deserts and frozen into the earth in Siberia. With her amazing talent for growing things, Roseli took tiny samples of these microbes home and grew more of them in her lab so scientists could study them.

After NASA landed the Viking probe on Mars in 1976, scientists studied the research Roseli contributed to to learn more about the kinds of life that might exist on a planet with such a harsh environment.

NOVEMBER 23, 1937–SEPTEMBER 4, 2005
PHILIPPINES → UNITED STATES OF AMERICA

"DRY VALLEYS ARE REGARDED AS THE CLOSEST TERRESTRIAL ANALOG TO MARTIAN OR OTHER EXTRATERRESTRIAL PLANETARY ENVIRONMENTS."
—ROSELI OCAMPO-FRIEDMANN

ILLUSTRATION BY SALLY CAULWELL

SAMANTHA POWER

DIPLOMAT

Nine-year-old Samantha felt nervous as she sat at her desk in her new school in the United States. She looked down at her clothes. She felt out of place in the dark-green cardigan and plaid skirt she'd worn at her Catholic school in Ireland. She made an effort to fit in, even practicing an American accent and learning baseball stats.

Samantha was afraid of how people would treat her if they thought she was different. But the longer she stayed in her new home, the more Samantha adjusted. She also noticed—and loved—that all sorts of people were able to live together peacefully in the US.

When Samantha was twenty-two, she decided to become a journalist. There was a terrible war happening in the southeastern European country of Bosnia. Samantha went there and wrote about the suffering she saw. It made her angry that countries, including the United States, didn't do more to stop the fighting and help people. She wrote a book about the way the world reacts when people kill other people because of their religion or **ethnicity**. The book won the Pulitzer Prize.

Years later, when Barack Obama became president, he remembered Samantha's book. He asked her to be the US **ambassador** to the United Nations and help decide how the US should act abroad. The choices were hard, but Samantha always tried to argue for what she believed would make the world a better place.

Today Samantha is a professor at Harvard University, where she teaches students the lessons she learned as a writer and **diplomat**.

BORN SEPTEMBER 21, 1970
IRELAND → UNITED STATES OF AMERICA

"PEOPLE WHO CARE, ACT, AND REFUSE TO GIVE UP MAY NOT CHANGE *THE* WORLD, BUT THEY CAN CHANGE MANY INDIVIDUAL WORLDS."
—SAMANTHA POWER

ILLUSTRATION BY SARAH LOULENDO

SANDRA CAUFFMAN

ELECTRICAL ENGINEER

O nce upon a time, there was a girl who dreamed of working for NASA. On a summer night in Costa Rica, Sandra watched the first moon landing on her neighbors' TV. The living room was packed with people, but as Neil Armstrong's boot touched the moon's surface, no one said a word. They were too amazed. "I walked home that night and looked at the moon so far away," Sandra said, "and I knew then that I wanted to be part of that adventure."

Sandra shared her dream with her mother right away. Sandra's family was poor, and her mother raised her family alone, working long hours at difficult jobs. But she saw the light in her daughter's eyes and encouraged her to work hard.

Sandra *did* work hard. She excelled in school and enrolled in a Costa Rican university. She wanted to study electrical engineering, but a professor told her it wasn't "ladylike," so she studied industrial engineering instead. In the middle of college, Sandra's family moved to the US. There, she was able to study electrical engineering (and physics), like she'd always wanted to, and earned her degree.

A few years later, Sandra achieved her childhood dream—she was hired by NASA. She became a NASA engineer, focusing on designing satellites and on space exploration—including missions to Mars! "I just finished launching a satellite to Mars," Sandra said in 2015. "It is just incredible that a little piece of me and a little piece of Costa Rica has traveled to Mars and is now orbiting the Red Planet."

BORN MAY 10, 1962
COSTA RICA ➔ UNITED STATES OF AMERICA

"WHEN I WAS SEVEN YEARS OLD,
I WANTED TO GO TO THE MOON.
LOOK WHERE I AM TODAY.
I HAVE LANDED AMONG THE STARS."
—SANDRA CAUFFMAN

SARA MAZROUEI

PLANETARY GEOLOGIST

Once there was a girl in Iran who wanted to blaze her own trail like a comet in the night sky. Sara spent her childhood marveling at outer space and reading books about brave girls who weren't afraid to be different. It was good training for what was to come.

When Sara was thirteen, her family moved to Canada so she and her sisters could study and be whatever they wanted. Things *were* different in Canada, but not all doors were open the way they'd hoped.

Sara dreamed of being a NASA scientist. While working on her PhD, she was chosen for a NASA internship, but a few weeks after she arrived, Sara received unexpected news: she didn't have security clearance to be at NASA because she had been born in Iran. The officials even questioned how she had gotten the internship. Sara was frustrated—she had been honest about her birthplace from the beginning.

Nevertheless, Sara's sense of adventure and her love of math and science propelled her to finish her internship, get her PhD, and become a planetary scientist. She went on to teach others about space and to study things including the history of asteroids and the best landing locations for future lunar missions. She also spoke out for equality. She believed that people should be free to be leaders in STEM careers, no matter their gender or where they're from. "I wonder how much more I could've achieved," Sara said, "if I didn't have to spend half of my time defending the fact that I belong where I am."

BORN NOVEMBER 3, 1987

IRAN ➡ CANADA

"WHY DOES IT MATTER WHERE YOU WERE BORN WHEN YOU'RE TRYING TO STUDY THINGS OUT OF THIS WORLD?"
—SARA MAZROUEI

ILLUSTRATION BY EVA RUST

SARA MCLAGAN

NEWSPAPER EDITOR

Sara was only a toddler when her family moved from Northern Ireland to Canada. Her father had been sent by the British government to take up a job there as an engineer.

Sara started working as a switchboard operator when she was about thirteen years old, and soon Western Union put her in charge of connecting all the messages that passed between her station in Matsqui, British Columbia, and the United States. Thick calluses grew on her fingertips from tapping out messages in Morse code, but Sara didn't care. She liked being part of the system that brought people information—and she was good at it. She eventually became an office manager, a job that few women held.

When Sara got married, her husband, John, wanted to start a brand-new newspaper: the *Vancouver Daily World*. He knew Sara was the perfect person to help.

Sadly, around 1901, John became very sick and died. Sara didn't want to see the paper shut down. Instead, she decided to run it herself. She managed the staff, wrote stories, and read over the pages to check for mistakes before they went to the printer. She also made sure that the paper ran articles on things that would be helpful to women who worked hard to care for their homes and families. She oversaw stories on topics such as health, child care, and nutrition. By taking on this important role, Sara became Canada's first-ever female newspaper publisher of a major daily paper.

CIRCA 1856–MARCH 20, 1924

IRELAND ➔ CANADA

ILLUSTRATION BY
BARBARA DZIADOSZ

SAU LAN WU

PHYSICIST

Once upon a time, there was a girl who slept in a rice shop. Sau Lan and her mother and brother lived in a crowded slum in Hong Kong, where there wasn't enough space in their apartment for everyone to lie down.

Growing up, Sau Lan first dreamed of becoming a painter. Then one day, she read a book about the great physicist and chemist Marie Curie, and changed her mind. She would become a scientist instead and search for a different kind of beauty in her work.

When it came time to go to university, Sau Lan knew her family could not afford to pay her tuition. Then she got a letter from Vassar College in New York. It offered her a full scholarship to study there.

After Vassar, Sau Lan went on to get a PhD in physics at Harvard University. She was fascinated by the tiny particles that made up atoms, which in turn made up everything else in the universe. Because they were so small, they were also very hard to study.

In 1974, Sau Lan's research team discovered a particle called J/psi, which helped scientists understand more about how matter works. Soon after, she helped discover gluon, a particle that holds parts of an atom together. Then she tackled one of the most important challenges in all of physics: the discovery of the Higgs boson, a particle so hard to find that many scientists were not even sure it existed. In 2012, Sau Lan's team found evidence that the Higgs boson was real— and to Sau Lan, it was beautiful.

BORN CIRCA 1941

HONG KONG ➡ UNITED STATES OF AMERICA

"TRY TO INNOVATE. NOTHING WILL BE EASY. BUT IT IS ALL WORTH IT TO DISCOVER SOMETHING NEW."
—SAU LAN WU

ILLUSTRATION BY
ADRIANA BELLET

SURYA BONALY

Once upon a time, a figure skater glided onto the ice in a beautiful, sparkling costume for a performance no one would ever forget. It was the 1998 Olympic Games in Nagano, Japan, and there had never been a skater like Surya. She could do things on the ice that hardly anyone else could: cartwheels, giant leaps, even a backflip. She won the French national championships nine times, the European championships five times (once with a broken toe), and three silver medals in the world championships. When Surya skated, she felt like she was making art on the ice.

Surya's most famous move—the backflip—was banned from the Olympics. Skaters weren't allowed to do flips in competition. But Nagano would be her last Olympic performance, and she didn't expect to win, so Surya didn't care what the judges said. She wanted to do something big and brave.

As the music soared, Surya did a backflip and landed on one foot! No skater in history had ever done that before—or since. The crowd went wild. They hurled flowers onto the ice. When the music stopped, Surya turned away from the judges, ignoring her scores, and bowed to the audience instead.

After the Olympics, Surya became a professional figure skater and coach, and eventually moved to the United States. Some estimated that she had done more than five hundred backflips in shows around the world. It was her signature move, and she was unstoppable.

BORN DECEMBER 15, 1973
FRANCE ➡ UNITED STATES OF AMERICA

"I DID MY BEST, BUT
I CAN ALWAYS DO BETTER."
—SURYA BONALY

SUSAN FRANCIA

ROWER

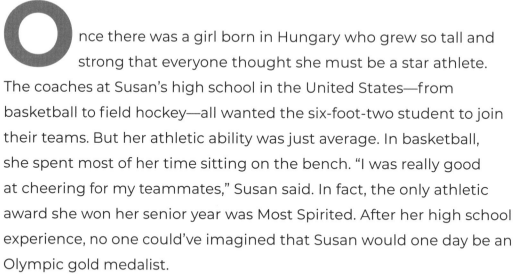

Once there was a girl born in Hungary who grew so tall and strong that everyone thought she must be a star athlete. The coaches at Susan's high school in the United States—from basketball to field hockey—all wanted the six-foot-two student to join their teams. But her athletic ability was just average. In basketball, she spent most of her time sitting on the bench. "I was really good at cheering for my teammates," Susan said. In fact, the only athletic award she won her senior year was Most Spirited. After her high school experience, no one could've imagined that Susan would one day be an Olympic gold medalist.

During her sophomore year of college, Susan joined her university's rowing team on a whim. She missed playing sports, and rowing was one of the only teams at her school that let anyone try out. Susan had never even held an oar. Yet when she and her teammates pulled the boat through the water, it felt like something she'd been born to do. Over the next few years, Susan became a powerful and determined rower. "For the first time, I didn't just have 'potential,'" Susan said. "I was actually excelling!"

Some of Susan's coaches encouraged her to try out for the Olympic team. After she graduated from college, that's exactly what she did. She not only made the Olympic team for the 2008 Beijing Summer Games but Susan and her teammates also won a gold medal! Four years later, at the Summer Olympics in London, she won a gold medal again. Afterward, Susan used her Olympic journey to inspire others.

BORN NOVEMBER 8, 1982

HUNGARY ➔ UNITED STATES OF AMERICA

ILLUSTRATION BY
KATHRIN HONESTA

"IT WAS AWESOME
TO FIND SOMETHING
WHERE I COULD
FINALLY LIVE UP
TO MY POTENTIAL."
—SUSAN FRANCIA

SUSAN POLGAR

CHESS CHAMPION

One day in Budapest, a little girl named Susan walked into a neighborhood chess club with her father. The men in the room were surprised to see the girl, but one of the men agreed to play her in a match. Later, the room was even more surprised when she won!

Susan was only four years old, but she was already training to be a chess champion. Her father, László, was a psychologist who studied child prodigies. He thought that any child could become a "genius" in a subject they put their mind to. Rather than send Susan and her sister to school, László taught them at home, training them to be expert chess players. The sisters studied chess for six hours a day!

In the 1970s, the world's best chess players were men. Some people thought this was proof that the female brain was unable to understand the game. But Susan and her sisters proved them wrong, winning matches against both women *and* men. By fifteen, Susan was the best female chess player in the world. In 1986, she became the first woman to qualify for the Men's World Chess Championship. She wasn't allowed to play that year, but the rules were later changed to allow women competitors.

Susan was a world-champion chess player four times, won ten medals in the Chess Olympiad, and was the first woman to earn the title of Grandmaster—the highest honor in chess—the same way men did. After moving to the US in 1994, she founded her own chess training center to teach the next generation of players.

BORN APRIL 19, 1969

HUNGARY ➔ UNITED STATES OF AMERICA

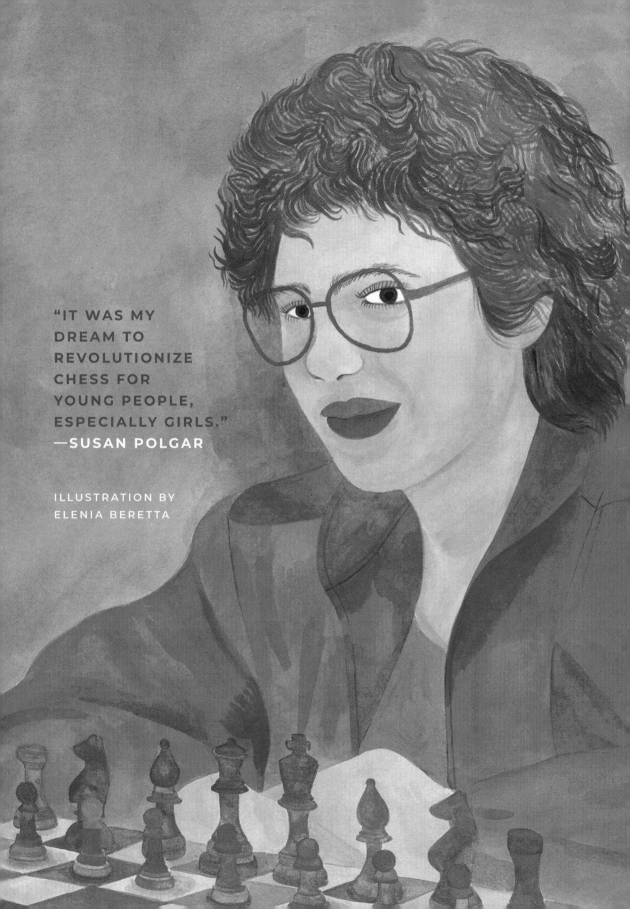

"IT WAS MY DREAM TO REVOLUTIONIZE CHESS FOR YOUNG PEOPLE, ESPECIALLY GIRLS."
—SUSAN POLGAR

ILLUSTRATION BY ELENIA BERETTA

TEREZA LEE

ACTIVIST

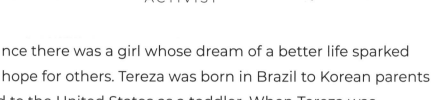

Once there was a girl whose dream of a better life sparked hope for others. Tereza was born in Brazil to Korean parents but moved to the United States as a toddler. When Tereza was still young, her father told her a secret: they were **undocumented** immigrants and not legal **citizens**.

Her family's secret made Tereza feel afraid all the time. Chicago was the only home she had ever known. But if the US government found out about her family, they could send them back to Brazil or South Korea.

Tereza channeled her energy into music and spent hours alone practicing the piano. Music gave her hope, and when she was in high school, she played Tchaikovsky Piano Concerto with the Chicago Symphony Orchestra.

When a teacher encouraged her to apply for college, Tereza shared her secret. They contacted their senator, Dick Durbin, who wrote a bill just for Tereza that would allow her to attend college. Soon other undocumented students heard about it and asked for help, too. Senator Durbin drafted a new bill called the DREAM Act. It would create a way for people who had arrived in the US as children to become citizens.

The bill was on its way to becoming law when the terrorist attacks of September 11, 2001, stopped it in its tracks. Today thousands of people are still working to pass the DREAM Act. What started as one girl's dream became a movement that helped others find their voice.

BORN JANUARY 12, 1983

BRAZIL ➜ UNITED STATES OF AMERICA

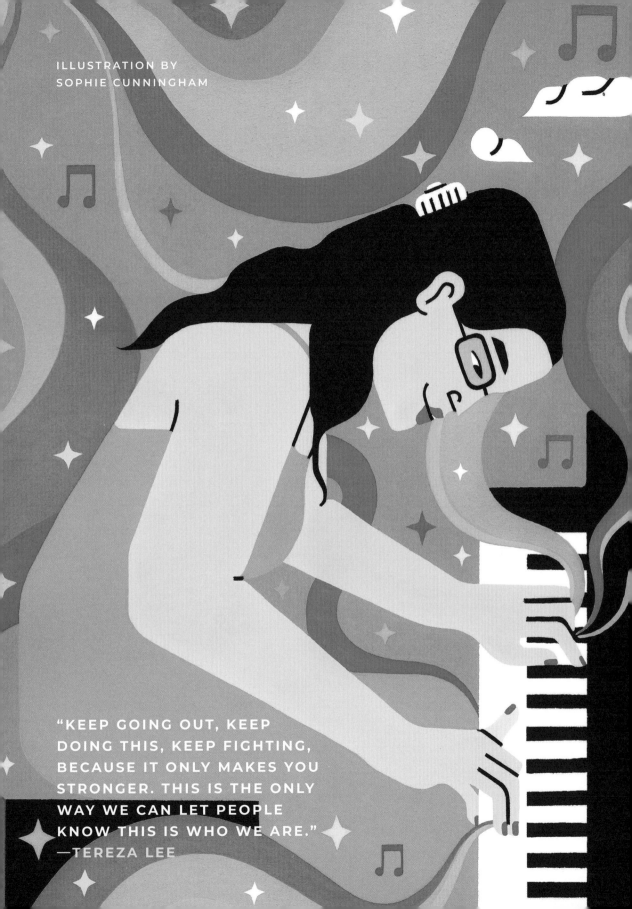

ILLUSTRATION BY
SOPHIE CUNNINGHAM

"KEEP GOING OUT, KEEP
DOING THIS, KEEP FIGHTING,
BECAUSE IT ONLY MAKES YOU
STRONGER. THIS IS THE ONLY
WAY WE CAN LET PEOPLE
KNOW THIS IS WHO WE ARE."
—TEREZA LEE

TIMNIT GEBRU

COMPUTER SCIENTIST

Once there was a girl who lived in a home filled with people who loved numbers and science. In Timnit's house in Ethiopia, when you encountered a problem, you found a way to fix it.

When Timnit was a teenager, war broke out between Ethiopia and Eritrea. People of Eritrean descent, like Timnit and her family, were being forced to flee. Her family left the country and found **asylum** in the United States.

When Timnit started high school in Massachusetts, she tried to enroll in the hardest math and science classes. To Timnit's confusion, the teacher discouraged her. This teacher didn't think a student from Africa could do high-level work. Timnit couldn't believe how ridiculous that was. She graduated as soon as she could and enrolled at Stanford University. By the time she left Stanford, she had a PhD in electrical engineering!

During her graduate studies, Timnit got interested in artificial intelligence. She saw that many computer programs came built-in with prejudices and biases. Those that recognized faces, for example, didn't work as well on people of color. If artificial intelligence was going to change the world for the better, Timnit realized, it had to be fair. The people who built these tools should look like the people who used them, so Timnit started programs to encourage women and people of color to study engineering.

Today Timnit works for Google to create ethical artificial intelligence programs.

ETHIOPIA → UNITED STATES OF AMERICA

"THERE IS NO SUCH THING AS A MATH
PERSON VERSUS NOT A MATH PERSON.
THAT'S SOCIETY TELLING YOU THERE IS
ONLY ONE TYPE OF PERSON FOR ONE FIELD."
—TIMNIT GEBRU

TURIA PITT

ATHLETE AND AUTHOR

Once there was a girl who was determined to overcome any obstacle in her path. Turia was born in Tahiti and grew up on a cliff overlooking the Pacific Ocean in Australia. Nearly every day before and after school, she'd surf the blue waves or run along the beach. She loved exploring the Australian landscape.

When it was time to choose a career, one option stood out: mining engineer. Turia loved science, math, and the outdoors. She was a problem solver and liked the idea of working in the remote Australian outback.

After she got her first engineering job, Turia ran an ultramarathon—one hundred kilometers through the outback. A few hours into the race, she was suddenly surrounded by a raging grassfire. Amazingly, Turia survived, but most of her body and face had been burned, and she lost several fingers. She was in the hospital for a long time.

Doctors told her she would never run again, but Turia didn't give up. Over the next two years, she relearned to walk, talk, and feed herself. Then she set bigger goals—and achieved those, too. After her accident, Turia completed two Ironman triathlons, hiked the Kokoda Trek, sailed around French Polynesia (the region where she was born), became a motivational speaker, launched a business, wrote three books, and became a mother. "I've rebuilt my life," Turia said, "and defied every expectation placed on me."

BORN JULY 25, 1987
TAHITI ➜ AUSTRALIA

ILLUSTRATION BY
LÉA TAILLEFERT
ROLLAND

"YOU ARE NOT LIMITED
BY WHAT OTHER
PEOPLE THINK OF YOU,
OR BY WHAT YOU THINK
OF YOURSELF!"
—TURIA PITT

VELMA SCANTLEBURY

TRANSPLANT SURGEON

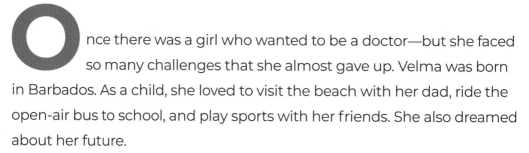

Once there was a girl who wanted to be a doctor—but she faced so many challenges that she almost gave up. Velma was born in Barbados. As a child, she loved to visit the beach with her dad, ride the open-air bus to school, and play sports with her friends. She also dreamed about her future.

When she was fifteen, Velma and her family moved to the United States. It was a very difficult time. At her new school in Brooklyn, Velma was teased about her hair, her accent, and her clothes. Even her school guidance counselor treated Velma differently from the other students. She told Velma that college wasn't for her and that she should get a job instead. "To her, I had no promising future," Velma said. "The darkness of my skin blinded her."

But Velma did get into college—and was awarded a full scholarship! She earned a biology degree and later attended medical school. Velma continued to face **discrimination**, but with the friendship and guidance of a female professor, she persevered. She also realized that she loved learning about surgery. In 1989, Velma became the first female African American transplant surgeon.

Velma has performed more than two thousand transplant surgeries and has won many awards for her work. She has also written a book and taught in order to share her knowledge with others. Velma works hard to address inequality in the medical field and to encourage girls to become surgeons even when it seems difficult.

BORN OCTOBER 6, 1955

BARBADOS → UNITED STATES OF AMERICA

ILLUSTRATION BY
IRENE RINALDI

"SURROUND YOURSELF
WITH POSITIVE PEOPLE WHO
ARE GOING TO LIFT YOU UP."
—VELMA SCANTLEBURY

XIYE BASTIDA PATRICK

ACTIVIST

Once upon a time, a terrible drought gripped Xiye's hometown of San Pedro Tultepec, Mexico. The land was parched. The lake dried up. Crops died. After two years, the rain finally came—but it wasn't a normal storm. It poured and poured until the land flooded.

Xiye belonged to the Otomi Toltec, a nation of Indigenous people. Her community understood the importance of living in balance with the environment and caring for the earth. When Xiye moved with her family to New York City, she saw the damage left by Hurricane Sandy and realized the balance was dangerously off. The climate was in crisis. She had to do something to make it right.

In March 2019, when she was seventeen years old, Xiye organized a strike at her high school in New York. Under her leadership, around six hundred students walked out of class to demand that governments take action to stop climate change and protect the planet. Months later, Xiye and other young activists around the world led a week of global strikes and protests for climate change and Indigenous rights.

To make time for her activism, Xiye had to give up gymnastics and other activities she loved. But the earth was worth it.

"Indigenous people have been taking care of the earth for thousands of years because that is their **culture**," Xiye said. "For me, being an environmental activist and a climate justice **activist** is not a hobby. It's a way of life."

BORN CIRCA 2002

MEXICO ➔ UNITED STATES OF AMERICA

"EARTH IS OUR HOME. IT GIVES YOU AIR, WATER, AND SHELTER. EVERYTHING WE NEED. ALL IT ASKS IS THAT WE PROTECT IT."
—XIYE BASTIDA PATRICK

ILLUSTRATION BY SALLY DENG

YOKY MATSUOKA

ROBOTICS ENGINEER

Once upon a time, there was a girl who dreamed with the intensity of a machine. In the beginning, she wanted to become a professional tennis player when she grew up. She moved to the United States at the age of sixteen and hoped to make it as a pro.

Unfortunately, Yoky suffered injury after injury and decided that a tennis career wasn't for her. Instead she found herself daydreaming: what if she built a robot that could play tennis with her whenever she wanted?

So Yoky went to the University of California, Berkeley, and studied robotics. She wanted to know how robots could help people. Yoky became a pioneer in the field of neurorobotics, studying the relationship between computers and the central nervous system.

Yoky eventually built mechanical arms that could help people learn to use their muscles again after a stroke. Her work was so creative, she received a prize called the MacArthur Fellowship—sometimes known as the genius grant.

Yoky wasn't the type of scientist to focus on just one project, though. She wanted to help people "become better versions of who they've always wanted to be." She was one of the first people to work at Google X, a top secret research department dedicated to solving hard problems. Then she helped start a company called Nest Labs and built a smart home thermometer. She went on to work for Google Health, which aims to use technology to change and save people's lives, and Panasonic.

BORN CIRCA 1972
JAPAN ➔ UNITED STATES OF AMERICA

"LIFE IS SHORT AND THERE ARE A LOT OF PEOPLE'S LIVES I WANT TO IMPROVE BECAUSE OF THINGS I CAN CONTRIBUTE IN A WAY THAT'S DIFFERENT FROM OTHERS."
—YOKY MATSUOKA

ILLUSTRATION BY LISA LANOË

YOSHIKO CHUMA

CHOREOGRAPHER AND PERFORMANCE ARTIST

When Yoshiko danced, wild things happened. She would leap around and stomp her boots on the floor. She left the stage and walked around the theater, or grabbed a chair and swung it over her head. Her performances were always different from anything audiences had seen before.

Yoshiko never took formal dance classes. As a girl in Osaka, Japan, Yoshiko had an elementary school teacher who taught students modern dance, and she was encouraged to learn more about the world outside their community. By the time Yoshiko went to university, she longed to travel.

A friend told her about a place that drew artists from all over the world: New York City. That's where Yoshiko decided to go. She did not speak English, but when she danced, she felt like she was communicating with her body.

Yoshiko's performances were a mix of modern dance and performance art. Sometimes audiences were confused. Yoshiko liked it that way. She started her own dance company named the School of Hard Knocks. That means learning things out in the real world, the way that Yoshiko did, instead of safely inside a classroom.

Yoshiko and her dance company have won many Bessie Awards, the highest honor for independent dancers in New York City. She has traveled to more than forty countries and worked with more than two thousand people to create her unique works of art.

BORN DECEMBER 25, 1950
JAPAN ➔ UNITED STATES OF AMERICA

ILLUSTRATION BY
ELENI DEBO

"I WISH MY AUDIENCE
WOULD NOT HAVE
EXPECTATIONS OR
PRECONCEPTIONS.
THEY LIMIT THE
IMAGINATION."
—YOSHIKO CHUMA

YOUNG JEAN LEE

PLAYWRIGHT

Once there was a girl who spent her childhood playing with dollhouses, moving the plastic people around like actors on a stage. Young Jean and her parents had left South Korea for the United States, eventually settling in a small town in Washington when she was just two years old. The town was an unfriendly place for Asian Americans. Throughout her childhood, Young Jean remembers being ashamed of her **culture**, even hiding the food they ate.

But her life changed when Young Jean moved to California for college. For the first time, she was surrounded by other Asian Americans. She had found a place where she could belong. Young Jean majored in English and spent years studying Shakespeare. She was fascinated by Shakespeare's plays and over-the-top characters. Young Jean soon realized something important: she didn't want to just study plays—she wanted to write them.

Young Jean started to read all the plays she could get her hands on. She even wrote to a well-known playwright for advice. She wanted to write plays for experimental theater, productions that didn't follow the typical rules and had unexpected elements. Young Jean began writing, attended graduate school, and later founded her own theater company to produce her work. To this day, she has continued to write plays that explore challenging topics such as race, identity, and politics.

In 2018, she became the first Asian American woman to have a play produced on Broadway.

BORN MAY 30, 1974
SOUTH KOREA → UNITED STATES OF AMERICA

ILLUSTRATION BY
SALINI PERERA

"I'M CONTINUALLY TRYING
TO CHALLENGE MYSELF...
TO ACTUALLY FACE THINGS THAT
MAKE ME UNCOMFORTABLE."
—YOUNG JEAN LEE

YUAN YUAN TAN

· · · · · · · · · · · · · · ·

BALLERINA

Yuan Yuan was a girl who loved music. Whenever she heard a song on the radio or television in her family's Shanghai apartment, her body would sway, and she'd find herself dancing in time with the rhythm. Her mother wanted to send her to ballet school.

"Absolutely not!" her father said. He wanted Yuan Yuan to become a doctor. Ballet was a distraction, he thought.

"We'll flip a coin," her mother said firmly.

Ten-year-old Yuan Yuan held her breath as the silver-colored five-cent coin tumbled through the air. When it landed, her mother's side was facing up. She was going to learn ballet!

Yuan Yuan eventually won many prizes at international ballet competitions for her graceful, elegant style. When she was eighteen, the artistic director of the San Francisco Ballet invited her to the US to dance as a guest star at the company's 1995 opening night gala. Afterward, that director asked her to stay and join the ballet company permanently.

Yuan Yuan soon became a principal dancer, one of the company's most senior and special ballerinas. She was the youngest principal dancer in the company's history and the first to come from Asia.

Yuan Yuan has danced the lead in the world's most famous ballets, including *Giselle*, *Swan Lake*, and *The Nutcracker*. In 2015, she celebrated her twentieth anniversary with the San Francisco Ballet with a special tour of performances in China—the place where her life as a ballerina began, all thanks to the flip of a coin.

· ·

BORN FEBRUARY 14, 1977

CHINA ➜ UNITED STATES OF AMERICA

ILLUSTRATION BY
PETRA BRAUN

"TO BE PERFECT IS IMPOSSIBLE,
BUT TO BE BETTER IS POSSIBLE.
WHEN I LOOK BACK AND SEE THAT
I'M BETTER THAN YESTERDAY,
THEN IT'S GOOD ENOUGH."
—YUAN YUAN TAN

ZAINAB SALBI

ACTIVIST

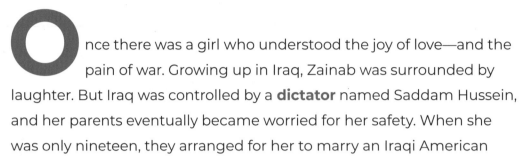

Once there was a girl who understood the joy of love—and the pain of war. Growing up in Iraq, Zainab was surrounded by laughter. But Iraq was controlled by a **dictator** named Saddam Hussein, and her parents eventually became worried for her safety. When she was only nineteen, they arranged for her to marry an Iraqi American man who lived in the United States.

This man turned out to be cruel. Zainab was all alone in an unfamiliar country. She could not go back to Iraq, but she also would not stay with a person who treated her badly.

Zainab escaped from her abusive husband. She took any job she could to support herself and studied for her university degree. In college, Zainab learned how war affected women all over the world, forcing them from their homes and endangering their lives. Now that she was safe, she wanted to help women who weren't.

When she was twenty-three, Zainab founded Women for Women International, a humanitarian organization that helps women survivors of war rebuild their lives. Zainab led this group for twenty years before she was ready for a new challenge. Stories could change people's lives, she thought. What if she helped women tell their own?

Zainab travels the world to interview female lawmakers, activists, and leaders. Her books, television shows, and documentaries encourage people to understand one another and have compassion for one another's experiences.

BORN SEPTEMBER 24, 1969

IRAQ ➜ UNITED STATES OF AMERICA

ILLUSTRATION BY
NOA DENMON

"NOT TO BE LIKE ANY MAN
BUT TO BE MYSELF. THAT'S
WHAT FEMINISM IS TO ME."
—ZAINAB SALBI

WRITE YOUR STORY

O nce upon a time, _____

_____

_____

_____

_____

_____

_____

_____

_____

_____

_____

_____

_____

_____

_____

_____

_____

_____

_____

_____

_____

_____

_____

_____

_____

DRAW YOUR PORTRAIT

GLOSSARY

ABOLITIONIST (noun) – a person who wants to end slavery

ACTIVIST (noun) – a person who campaigns to create social or political change

ALLIES (noun) – the group of countries that came together to oppose the Axis powers (Germany, Italy, Japan) during World War II

AMBASSADOR (noun) – a person sent to another country as a representative of their government

ANCESTOR (noun) – a person who was part of one's family several generations ago

ASYLUM (noun) – protection granted by a nation

CITIZEN (noun) – a native or naturalized member of a state or nation

CULTURE (noun) – the shared characteristics of a society or group of people, including food, clothing, language, customs, beliefs, and religion

DICTATOR (noun) – a single ruler who has complete authority over a country

DIPLOMAT (noun) – a person whose job is to keep good relations between the governments of different countries

DISCRIMINATION (noun) – the unfair treatment of a person or group in a certain category, especially based on race, age, gender, or religion

DISPLACED PERSON (noun) – a person who is forced to leave their home and/or country

EMIGRATE (verb) – to leave one's country in order to permanently live in another

ETHNICITY (noun) – identity with a certain racial, national, or cultural group

HOLOCAUST (noun) – the massacre of civilians on a large scale, especially Jewish people, that took place during World War II

JUDO (noun) – a martial art of unarmed combat intended to train the body and mind; a modified form of jujitsu (a Japanese method of defending oneself by using strength and weight instead of weapons); the word combines the Japanese characters *jū*, meaning "gentleness," and *do*, meaning "art"

IMMIGRATE (verb) – the act of coming to a country to live there permanently

LEGACY (noun) – something handed down from the past; a person's mark on the world that lives on after they stop working or pass away

ORTHOPEDIC (adjective) – a word used to describe treatment of muscles, bones, or joints

PHILANTHROPY (noun) – the act of helping others on a large scale

PREJUDICE (noun) – a judgment of someone based on external characteristics before knowing anything about them

PROTESTERS (noun) – a group of people who publicly demonstrate that they are opposed to something (for example, a law)

RACISM (noun) – a belief that certain racial groups possess qualities that make them superior or inferior to others

REFUGEE (noun) – a person who is forced to leave their country because of war, exile, or natural disaster

RESISTANCE (noun) – a group of people within the same country, such as the French Resistance and the Dutch Resistance, who joined forces to work against Nazi rule during World War II

REVOLUTION (noun) – when people attempt to overthrow a government

SEGREGATION (noun) – the act of isolating or separating a race, class, or group from others

SUFFRAGE (noun) – the right to vote in an election

UNDOCUMENTED (adjective) – lacking the appropriate immigration or working papers

YIDDISH (noun) – a language written in Hebrew characters used by Jewish people of central and eastern European origin

ILLUSTRATORS

· · · · · · · · · · · · · · · · ·

Seventy extraordinary artists who identify as women and come from all over the world portrayed the trailblazing Rebel figures included in this book. Here are all of them!

ACKNOWLEDGMENTS

This book would not exist without my team at Rebel Girls. Thank you Michon, Giulia, Ele, Pam, Maithy, Grace, Cesar, Lisa, Annalisa, Karen, Emilio, Jes, Mel, Ashley, Rachel, Kristen, Lauren, Montse, Marina, and Megan. You all made this book possible by believing in me and in our shared mission. Thank you too, to Corinne, Andrea, Christine, Elizabeth, Ariana, and Marisa. I will be forever grateful.

To the Rebel Girls who continue to read and share our stories—now in nearly 50 languages!—and to the Rebel moms, dads, aunts, uncles, cousins, teachers, librarians, and friends who read along with them: you are the reason I started this movement in the first place. You inspire me to push toward a more just world every day.

To my parents, Angelo and Lucia, improbable and irresistible, and always united when it counts. To my friends, thank you for never hesitating. You have made me stronger and freer. To my all-star D.C. team, Lin, Mandy, and Deneen: you're my heroes!

To all the people who have helped me along my journey as an immigrant in the United States: thank you for making this land, my land.

ABOUT THE AUTHOR

· · · · · · · · · · · · · · · · · ·

ELENA FAVILLI is a *New York Times* bestselling author, journalist, and breaker of glass ceilings. Elena is the founder and Chief Creative Officer of Rebel Girls, a media company dedicated to inspiring the next generation of brave and confident girls. In 2016, she co-wrote and published the most crowdfunded literary project in history, *Good Night Stories for Rebel Girls*, now translated into nearly 50 languages. She has written for the *Guardian*, *Vogue*, *COLORS* magazine, *McSweeney's*, *RAI*, *Il Post*, and *La Repubblica*. She lives in Los Angeles with her dog Lafayette, a Bracco Italiano.

REBEL GIRLS is the preeminent educational entertainment company that empowers girls to pursue their dreams without limits. Rebel Girls products inspire girls to dream bigger and realize their fullest potential, by introducing them to extraordinary women throughout history. Stories are brought to life through book publishing, podcasts, toys, and digital media. The Rebel Girls community spans over 85 countries, with 5.5 million books sold in 49 languages and 6 million podcast downloads.

Timbuktu and Rebel Girls' products have won:

- 2020 Webby People's Voice Winner in Podcasts: Family & Kids
- 2020 Gold in Education at the New York Festivals Radio Awards
- 2020 Best Use of Content in a Social Context, Corporate Content Awards
- 2019 #1 Podcast in Education, People's Choice Podcast Awards
- 2018 Australian Book Industry Award for International Book
- 2018 Star Watch Superstars, *Publishers Weekly*
- 2017 Book of the Year, Blackwell's
- 2017 Book of the Year, Foyles
- 2016 *Play 60, Play On* (an initiative by the NFL foundation to reinvent public playgrounds)
- 2014 First Special Mention at Bordeaux Biennale of Architecture
- 2013 Best Children's Magazine of the Year at London Digital Magazine Awards
- 2012 Best Design Award at Launch Education and Kids
- 2012 Best Italian Startup

Join the Rebel Girls' community on:
Facebook: facebook.com/rebelgirls
Instagram: @rebelgirls
Twitter: @rebelgirlsbook
Web: rebelgirls.com

If you liked this book, please take a moment to review it wherever you prefer!

DISCOVER EVEN MORE INCREDIBLE REBELS!

MEET THE EXTRAORDINARY REAL-LIFE HEROINES OF THE REBEL GIRLS CHAPTER BOOK SERIES!

Uncover the groundbreaking inventions of Ada Lovelace, one of the world's first computer programmers.

Learn the exciting business of Madam C. J. Walker, the hair care industry pioneer and America's first female self-made millionaire.

Explore the thrilling adventures of Junko Tabei, the first female climber to summit Mount Everest.

Discover the inspiring story of Dr. Wangari Maathai, the Nobel Peace Prize-winning environmental activist from Kenya.

Follow the awe-inspiring career of Alicia Alonso, a world-renowned prima ballerina from Cuba.